ARRESTED
From Bad Habits to Breakthrough

Tony Leaner

Visit Y-NOT Publishing's Web site at www.y-notpublishing.com

Arrested: From Bad Habits to Breakthrough
Copyright© September 2012 by Y-NOT Publishing

No part of this publication may be reproduced, stored in a retrieval system, or transmitted in any form by any means - electronic, mechanical, photocopy, recording, or otherwise - without the prior permission of the publisher, except as provided by U.S.A. copyright law. For information, contact Y-NOT Publishing

Edited by Laura Jackson
Designed by Patricia A. Jackson

ISBN-10: 0984980059
ISBN-13: 978-0-9849800-5-5

Y-NOT Publishing
12138 Central Avenue
Suite 197
Mitchellville, MD 20721
www.y-notpublishing.com

Printed in the United States of America

Mitchellville, MD

Contents

Dedication
Acknowledgments
Introduction

1 The Account	11
2 How Did I Get Here?	17
3 Connecting the Dots	27
4 The Power of the Pew	39
5 If There is Anything I Can Do, Seriously...	49
6 We are Family	53
7 My Lady and Myself	57

Interviews with Ex-Offenders 65
  ~ David Dawson
  ~ Richard Melton
  ~ Vincent McKenzie
  ~ Larry Bussell
  ~ Van Whitfield

In Closing	101
Resources	103

Dedication

It is with great joy, trepidation, passion and relief that I present to you my book Arrested.

I dedicate this work to all of us who, for some reason or another, haven't taken proper care of ourselves. This eclectic group includes those of us who haven't put doctor's visits and checkups on the front burner of our lives. We know the risk and the penalty for such behavior but choose to flirt with the laws of health and health care. We're almost waiting for some extreme event to happen. We're waiting until we are ARRESTED! In essence, we're failing ourselves.

Acknowledgments

I couldn't have completed this project without God and several key people whom I'd like to thank.

To the Y-Not Publishing team of Pat Jackson, Laura Jackson and Linda Nivens: Thank you for making this journeyman's project so seamless and enjoyable. A special thanks goes out to my sister Phyllis and her daughter Adrinne for the research they conducted for the Resources section of this book. And to Tonya Bell, I thank you for your dedication in getting this booked released.

I'll be forever grateful for all of the many friends and relatives who encouraged me to put this life event in a book in hopes that it might impact men and perhaps change how we look at our health. Men die every day simply because we won't do the most basic, minimal things to take care of ourselves. This now has become an assignment for me. Thank you for joining me in this mission to create a paradigm shift in men's health and save lives.

A very special thank you goes to my medical team:
Dr. Robert Lowery, Cardiac & Thoracic Surgeon, Washington Hospital Center.

The entire Washington Hospital Center nursing staff, which took exceptional care of me for 10 days. You're truly called to nursing, and I appreciate the care you provided me and my family.

Dr. Harvey Katzen and his team Tracy and Barbara.
Milo and Francine from Cardio Rehab, all at Doctors Community Hospital.
Dr. Snyder and his team, Eric, Tiffany, Semi, Eleanor, Lucy, Dee, Doris and Esete, who made 35 radiation treatments bearable and drama-free.

Dr. Wayne Koch, cancer specialist/surgeon, Johns Hopkins Hospital.

I know God handpicked all of you for this time in my life, and I'm grateful to Him for selecting you just for me!

And finally I want to thank my wife Deborah, the driving force and CEO of Y-Not Publishing, who stood by me even at death's door and never wavered in her faith in God first and in me that I could fight this fight and then tell the story. I could never imagine life without you, and I thank God every day for blessing me with you.

Introduction

I was arrested in my early twenties in Chicago. A guy from the local precinct called me one day and said I needed to come down and address some unpaid parking tickets. I told the guy what time I would come down to the station and went on about my morning.

I never heard the word "warrant" or "arrest" in the conversation -- but I did know that the city of Chicago didn't play when it came to issuing parking tickets. That's why I had so many. I'd filed all my parking tickets in the glove compartment of my car. My way of dealing with the problem was just to add any new ones to my growing collection.

I went to the police station, asked for the guy who called me and went to his office. Five minutes later, the detective started the process of booking me. He planned to arrest me and put me in jail for parking tickets! It didn't matter that I didn't understand why I was going to jail. Ignorance of the law was no defense. I had broken the law – and it was time to pay. I escaped jail that day by posting a $25 bail. I paid the tickets, and ultimately the police dropped the charges.

I wish my second arrest had gone that well. I wish I'd remembered that ignorance of the law is no defense. No, I was about to learn this principle all over again and the cost for this arrest -- cardiac arrest -- was going to be greater than a simple $25 bail. No, this time my life would flash before me. This time I would have to give an account for my reckless behavior.

CHAPTER ONE
The Account

Like most guys, I thought my health was okay. In December 2011, I learned I was mistaken.

I had a procedure near the end of the month to remove a nodule on the back of my neck that had become cancerous. I stayed overnight in the hospital for observation and came home the next day, but I didn't feel well.

I made some phone calls and talked to the staff of the hospital where I had surgery. My doctors had stressed to me: If you feel anything, go get it checked out. I just felt in my spirit that something wasn't right. In the process of getting examined at a nearby emergency room, a doctor calmly told me: "You're having a heart attack."

My Rap Sheet

I'm a guy who did all the wrong things with my health through the years -- and I've got the scars and the arrest record to prove it.

I'm a cancer survivor. I have diabetes. And my heart attack in December 2011 led to a triple bypass surgery. In fact, I'm still in treatment for some of my health issues.

Tony Leaner

My heart attack happened because I didn't really take care of myself. I didn't watch for the warning signs. I didn't listen to my wife when she would prod me to go to the doctor. And I didn't even listen to the doctor when I was diagnosed with diabetes. I didn't understand the association between diabetes and heart disease.

I never realized, or really took to heart, the correlation between my family history and health, and how that would ultimately have an impact on me. My lack of understanding almost cost me my life. After I came out of my triple bypass surgery, the doctors and my family told me I died twice on the table, but the surgeon revived me.

Silent but Deadly

Doctors call things like diabetes and heart disease silent killers. I truly believe that now. I had no sign that I had any issues. In fact, my heart surgeon told me that 60 percent of the people who have heart attacks never know they have a heart issue, problem or disease.

My diet was a major contributor to how I got here. My wife and I would share a meal, and I would get an extra order of fries. I'm diabetic, and I would have three or four cups of the sweetened iced tea. I ate desserts whenever I wanted to eat them. I would justify having what I wanted to have. I did everything I was big and bad enough to do. And I had plaque implode off my right artery.

What about exercise? In my mind, work was exercise. If I went to work and worked hard, and then played a couple rounds of golf, I was exercising. As men we can't understand why we're winded when we're playing softball or basketball during our family reunions. It's because we don't have the regiment in place to build stamina and protect our health.

Listening to My Body

I thank God that I had started listening to my body after my initial surgery for skin cancer in December 2011. If I had listened to my mind, my ego and my pride telling me I was okay, I might have gone to bed that night in December and died in my sleep.

Unlike many men, I didn't have any of the classic warning signs of a heart attack. I didn't have numbness in my arm. I didn't have dizziness or chest pains. All I felt was some slight discomfort, like the way you would feel if you slept on your arm the wrong way.

I'd started paying attention to my body, but it was almost too little, too late. Today I've got a scar where the surgeon opened my chest up to get to my heart and do the triple bypass surgery. I'd always wanted to go on a helicopter ride, but the only helicopter ride I've ever been on was the one from my local hospital to Washington Hospital Center in Washington, DC. Medical personnel rushed me into emergency surgery to put in a stent to remove 90 percent of the blockage in my right artery.

God has been good to me, and I now have a mandate. I'm giving men, regular guys like me, a call to action. We're not taking care of our health properly. We don't make our doctor's appointments like we should. I could have used a more common-sense approach to my health. Had I done that, I could have avoided some of the things that happened to me. Instead, I had to face arrest once again because I didn't know or seriously consider the law of health.

A Man's Man

Why didn't I yield to the many warnings and precautions related to my health? Because I'm a man –- that's man with a capital M -- and we just don't roll that way. We don't respond to information the way women do. When we hear something, especially something we don't want to hear… well let's just say it doesn't register in a way that makes a positive impact on our decision-making process.

My friend Van is the same way. Van told me a story the other day about when he experienced a major health crisis. He went to the hospital for a medical assessment. Then he left the hospital and went home -- only to be taken back to the hospital and admitted later that same night. He was in a coma for 30 days. Leaving the hospital and going home nearly cost Van his life. We will hear Van's story later on in this book.

Under a Death Sentence

I'm not qualified to jack you up about your health habits. I don't have a medical degree, and I'm not the poster boy for good health. I'm just a guy who experienced warnings, handcuffs and arrest for the crime of poor health. I served time and I'm now rehabilitated from my bad habits.

Now I'm sounding the alarm so you won't have to go through what I've gone through. If you don't arrest your bad habits -- your bad habits will arrest you.

I might have done things differently if I'd had this information earlier. I realize I need the straight facts, but I also need time to process information. I also need follow up, support and accountability.

I want to present this information in a way that will inspire us as men to re-examine our attitudes toward our health. We don't have to live under a death sentence. In fact, according to cardiologists, we can avoid or reverse some of the things that happen to us health-wise. But we have to make the right choices.

Choose Life

Romans 12:1 says that we're to present our bodies a living sacrifice. That's a decision we make -- a choice. We have to exercise. That's a choice, a tough choice. Although I've had a heart attack and a triple bypass operation, I still struggle every day in making the right choices. When I go out to a restaurant, the old me wants to eat what the old me ate before the cardiac arrest. At 6:00 a.m., the old me doesn't want to get out of the bed for my three-mile walk.

I fight daily to keep the commitments I made while I was on my back for three months recovering. But I swore I wouldn't go back in the hospital again for the same thing that put me in there the first time.

Tony Leaner

The Difference

I have the memories of the pain and struggle that I went through during my illness. Some of us have memories of similar or even worse experiences, and we still won't do the right things. We've been given another shot at life -- even if it is with some restrictions. Here's what has helped me. Get an accountability partner. Yep, someone who will walk with you or go to your doctor's appointments with you. Someone you trust to help you make the right choices.

If you're a baby boomer you should remember the Lone Ranger. Did he attempt to go it all alone? Nope, even the Lone Ranger had Tonto! So buddy up, partner up, man up and let's get this health thing moving in the right direction.

CHAPTER TWO
How Did I Get Here?

I didn't just wake up one day and have a heart attack, triple bypass surgery or cancer. The bad habits that led to my major health conditions started back in Chicago even as a child.

The South Side

I grew up on the South Side of Chicago, a major part of the city. Although it has endured a reputation as being poor or crime-infested, for me the South Side was home to the affluent and the working class, as well as to impoverished neighborhoods such as Englewood, Chatham and South Shore. Neighborhoods ran the gamut from the affluent Pill Hill, which is where all the doctors lived, to housing projects such as Cabrini-Green and Argyle Gardens, the latter being where President Barack Obama got his first real start as a community activist.

I grew up in Englewood where my family owned their home. This area tended to be composed of more blue-collar residents, while Hyde Park (where President Obama and his family lived) the Jackson Park Highlands District, Kenwood and Beverly attracted middle, upper-middle class and affluent residents. Englewood was a great place to grow up. I was never in any real trouble. I think the worst thing that happened to me was when I faced possible jail time for those unpaid parking tickets.

I remember my father being the chairman of the Englewood Conservation Committee. I'm not sure what that meant, but he served at the pleasure of the late mayor Richard M. Daley. All I know is that we got a Christmas card from the mayor every year and my Dad received invitations to a lot of functions. Our family joke was that position meant everything because when the city built the Dan Ryan Expressway (which came right down the middle of my neighborhood), the city built it toward the east and not the west, where our house stood, because my father was the chair of that committee!

I love Chicago. That city exposed me to a cultural and social lifestyle, professional sports teams, landmark buildings, nationally renowned museums, elite educational institutions, world class medical institutions and major parts of the city's elaborate parks. People used public transportation to get around, such as, The 'L' train via the Chicago Transit Authority and a number of Metro lines.

Chicago also has unique cuisine. Chicago pizza, rib tips or Italian beef, you can't find these foods anywhere else. We grew up on Rossi's pizza on the South side. It was the only place that delivered. Rossi's was a very thin crust pizza cut in little pieces.

Then you have the rib tips. When my brother Eric

and his wife Deb cooked out for the Fourth of July in 2012, there wasn't a rib anywhere in the house other than these rib tips. He bought a whole case and put them on the grill. You would think he was doing nice slabs of spare ribs, but they were tiny –- the ends, the top, the parts of the rib that others might have thrown away. This is what poor blacks often got back in the day, the parts of the pig or the cow nobody else wanted. Man were those tips good!

Italian beef, indigenous to Chicago, is just delicious. It's cooked in a broth with all the bay leaves and oregano. You could find Al's Italian Beef shops all over Chicago. In fact, when I would fly into Midway Airport to visit my family, I would make sure I detoured by one of Al's shops either when I landed or on my way back out of town.

Entertainers Around the Table

My family was nested in entrepreneurship. Back in the day, my great-grandparents owned a general store in Gowdy, Mississippi. When the local lumber factory decided they didn't want to handle the mail for their employees, that operation moved to my great-grandparents' store.

Years ago my family migrated to Chicago, as many blacks did, for a better life. Ultimately my father, Ernie, and his brother George started the only black-owned phonograph record distributing company, United Record Distributing Co. My mother, Jeanne, a stay-at-home mom during most of my developmental years, concentrated on raising me, my older brother Bill and my younger siblings, Phyllis and Eric.

In the 60's the music business was large and in charge

in Chicago, and my family was steeped in the middle of that movement. My dad had his corporate office in downtown Chicago and had stores called Record World throughout the South and North side. We even had a record store in downtown Chicago.

We rubbed shoulders with all kinds of entertainers, so something was always going on at my house or in the family. My great-uncle, Al Benson, was a pioneer in black radio in Chicago. So our Apollo Theater or Howard Theater was called the Regal Theater, and my uncle put those shows on. When the Motown Revue came to town, we went to the Regal to my great-uncle's shows. Even as a kid, I was able to meet Redd Foxx, Moms Mabley. You would see this revue -- whoever was touring at the time.

My dad distributed a lot of these artists in the Midwest, groups like the Shirrelles, who had the song title "Will You Still Love Me Tomorrow." Smokey Robinson, Chuck Jackson -- these artists would have five shows on Saturday or Sunday. In between shows they would come to my parents' home for gumbo or chili. We always had a pot simmering -- a huge pot of whatever it was. You couldn't even see the bottom.

The joke in Chicago was you could get a drink before you could get a meal. But if you went to somebody's house at the right time, you could find a pot simmering -- northern beans or black eyed peas. Or somebody was having a cookout.

The weekend was the time to party with good food and plenty to drink. My Dad, my uncle, my older brother Bill and many of Bill's employees would come to the house after work on Fridays and we would party all weekend, eating anything we were big and bad enough to eat. Sunday dinner was big too. We went to church, came home and had Sunday dinner. That was every Sunday.

We ate traditional Southern cooking because lots of people in Chicago had come up from the South. But half of my family had what we called "sugar," diabetes or high blood sugar. My dad had it. My great-uncle was a double amputee who had lost both of his legs due to complications from diabetes. Several of my relatives struggled with their health, but they still ate whatever they wanted to eat. As far as I could tell there were no restrictions on any food choices. That was my model from diabetics: you just lived with the disease.

Move to Maryland

Some years later I met my beautiful bride on the North side of Chicago. We moved to Maryland and got married. I was ready to embrace life on the East Coast: the great seafood, a job outside of the family business, church, a new wife and son and, for the first time, making doctor's visits a priority.

See, I had gone through life pretty much unscathed when it came to my health. I remember chipping a front tooth when I was around 6 or 7, and fracturing a baby toe in my mid-twenties, but other than that, I never really had any other health issues.

That is, until 1993 when I was diagnosed with diabetes in Maryland. All I could think about was how did I get here? I felt I had lost the battle of life. I actually got depressed, and I remember talking with my wife and my father about those feelings.

Tony Leaner

I began taking my medicine and doing what I could to get my blood sugar under control. I went through life always chasing after that preverbal 'good' blood sugar number but never with much success. As I think about it now, I don't think I really took my diagnosis seriously, and I drifted back into my regular eating habits. This is where it all started for me.

Tony Leaner

ARRESTED: From Bad Habits to Breakthrough

United Record Distributors

Tony's Parents with Diana Ross

Tony Leaner

Tony's Dad with Smokey Robinson

Tony's Dad with President Jimmy Carter

ARRESTED: From Bad Habits to Breakthrough

Jackson 5

Tony with Sister Sledge & Tom Joyner

Tony Leaner

Tony's Dad (Ernie) & Uncle George

CHAPTER THREE
Connecting the Dots

Lying in a hospital bed trying to recover from major surgery forced me to look back over my life. I wasn't playing the blame game. My doctor had told me I had Type 2 diabetes. He told me how to change my diet, and he stayed on my case about eating right and bringing my sugar level down. But there was a disconnect somewhere. What did I miss when my doctor initially diagnosed me with diabetes at age 42? How did my inability to change my lifestyle and diet land me in the hospital 14 years later?

Eating Well but Not Healthy

My dad had a cerebral hemorrhage, a stroke, at age 68. As far as I know, no man in my family has ever seen 70. I'm 62, and my health crises began at 61. My brother and I both said, wow, here's a pattern. Am I cursed? No, I cursed myself. I was doing the same things my family did, and I wasn't sticking to the health habits they should have followed.

    My dad had a stroke. One of my uncles had cancer. I had an aunt who had a stroke. But I never made a direct correlation between their strokes and my diabetes. Now that I look back, they all struggled. They ate whatever they wanted to eat. My mom was the bomb cook but my dad also cooked. And not just one dish. My dad made the best neck bones. My dad was from Jackson, and those Mississippi folks could throw down. The men cooked, so there was a double pattern.

My dad had a business to run, however, so I would watch my mom cook while I was sitting in the kitchen doing homework or something (I was always in trouble for something as the middle child). Once I got older I learned other tricks from my dad, but when I was growing up, I always watched my mom. And she and my relatives would bake cakes and pies. My mom made the best lemon meringue pie. German chocolate cake –- I can still taste the chocolate and the nuts. It was about love and nurturing. Growing up in Chicago, you didn't go out in the winter without breakfast, even if it was toast or oatmeal.

My mom would make a roast beef shoulder or something, and we would eat. The big thing was to be able to go back and make a roast beef sandwich on white bread with mayonnaise. So the model for me was never set on eating in a healthy way. The model was eating well. And the Leaner's ate well.

I remember my grandfather worked in the stockyard. I don't know if it was part of the deal, but he would come home with the biggest hams and turkeys. You always had vegetables and stuff too –- greens and sweet potatoes. My aunt, the same diabetic aunt who had the stroke, she liked the sweet potatoes with marshmallows on top. If you made candied yams without the marshmallows, it wouldn't taste right to her. She made the best coconut cake. And at Christmas time, three or four candy dishes would overflow with all kinds of colorful treats.

My father's mother had a deep freezer in the kitchen. You could have put a body in that freezer. One side would have meats, and the other side would hold desserts. They would make macaroni and cheese and yams and brown-and-serve rolls lapped with butter. Grits with butter. That's how I grew up.

So when doctors told me I had diabetes, the news went over my head. My first thought was, "Man, it caught up with me too," but within a year I went back to eating what I normally ate. My doctor did everything he was supposed to do to help me change my diet. During my follow-up visits in the early 90s, he would say, "Tony, your numbers are off the scale. You gotta do better." I wasn't exercising, and I ate everything I wanted to eat, the same types of food I ate as a child. My family would say, "Oh, wow, if dad were here, he would be really proud. That hash you made tasted just like his."

When my mom died, my only request from her estate was her cookbooks. There are volumes of tried-and-true dishes. My mom was a phenomenal cook. Everybody thinks their mom can burn, but my mom's chili was legendary, world-renowned. In Chicago, you served chili over spaghetti with oyster crackers. You could have cheese and onions on the side but you didn't need it with my mom's chili. And it was spicy. People just couldn't get over her chili.

She was an international cook as well. She figured out how to make Chicken tetrazzini with a cream sauce, mushrooms and pasta and the right layer of cheese on the top. She could make Chinese food. We order Chinese food from a restaurant, but when she was putting on the Ritz, she would make pepper steak and fried rice. Who does this?

The showstopper was gumbo once or twice a year. Their gumbo was different than most because this was Chicago. It would have oysters, chicken, ham, and beef -- all kinds of stuff. People from Louisiana said, "You must be from New Orleans," because she knew how to do the roux. When I made gumbo for Thanksgiving 2011, I used turkey and her roux recipe.

Games People Play

But diet was only part of our issue with poor health. The adults in my life modeled other kinds of risky behavior that led me to take my own health for granted.

I didn't take heart attack as a major thing. I didn't understand the gravity of having a heart attack. I weighed about 200 pounds, but I carried it well and I was somewhat active with golf. I typically wore custom-made clothes. Even if I bought something off the rack, I wore clothes tailored just for me. So if you just looked at me, you might not have guessed what was going on with my health. But the extra weight wasn't good for me. Plus I had wrestled with cholesterol for years.

At one of my favorite steakhouses, for example, you can get a little dab of butter on top of your sizzling steak.

I would ask for extra butter. So I was eating red meat with butter, and I'm eating the butter twice. Plus this restaurant makes the best fries. I didn't need a salad. Man, give me the meat and potatoes.

What's worse, I wasn't measuring my blood sugar daily prior to my heart attack. My great-uncle, who had wrestled with diabetes, lost one leg and then later the other one. He was a vibrant guy, a tough cookie, who wound up coming to family events in a wheelchair. I saw the devastating effects of this disease on his life, but I still took my diabetes lightly.

One time my dad came to Maryland to visit me and my wife. During his visit, we went out to eat stuffed flounder and all kinds of food at some of the best local seafood restaurants. The nights we didn't go out, my dad would stay home and fry fish or cook something else. Eventually my dad starting getting headaches that would force him to rest until his blood sugar could come down. This was before he got on the needle.

After going on the needle, my dad would take an extra shot of insulin when he knew he was going to eat something he shouldn't eat. Similarly, my mom, who had high blood pressure, would skip her medication if she planned to have a cocktail.

I didn't make those kinds of choices, but my health habits were just as bad. I'd eat three quarters of a slice of cake but avoid eating the icing on the large end of the slice. I thought I was looking out for myself, but I didn't consider that I'd eaten the two layers of icing in the middle of the slice.

My older brother, meanwhile, feared the dentist. Like many men, he avoided the pain and uncertainty of going to a medical professional, and his teeth were in terrible shape as a result.

I had a great uncle, Harold Johnson, in Las Vegas, who became ill several years ago. He owned a furniture store, and he introduced me to golf. I thought he died from prostate cancer. But when I talked to the young lady who managed his furniture store, she said that she would see blood in the store's only restroom. "But he never mentioned it," she said, "and I would try to figure out a way to say, hey, is everything okay?"

Lessons Learned

So after a lifetime of good eating that was bad for my body, a lifetime of risky behavior, the takeaway is this: I don't regret how I grew up. That was my childhood. But if I want to be on this earth for a while longer –- and I died twice while I was on the operating table –- I've got to change. I want to be around to enjoy my grandchildren. In fact, I've got two great-grandchildren I haven't seen yet because they live in Colorado. I have to shift how I look at my life. I've got to connect the dots to see how my past affects my present and future.

I'm also learning to make these changes:

I understand where I am physically. Coming back from this horrible experience, I feel older, wiser. I recognize I don't have the same stamina. We attended a football party not long ago, and at 9:30 p.m. my wife and I laughed because we knew it was close to our bedtime. Even if I'm still awake reading or watching the news at 11:00 p.m. or midnight, I'm at home.

ARRESTED: From Bad Habits to Breakthrough

Years ago, I wouldn't leave the house until 10:00 p.m.

But to have any kind of longevity, I have to make a mental shift. And it's hard. I don't want to get up at 6:00 a.m. and walk three miles. I would rather hit the snooze button. Even after what I've experienced, I still hesitate when someone asks: Do you want cheese on that breakfast sandwich? The old Tony wonders: Can I get away with it today? Can I sneak in a few chips? I've learned to eat before I leave the house so I don't wind up getting an extra large order of fries in some fast food drive-thru. Some of the food in those places can really ruin your health, but you can get a quick meal that tastes familiar.

I've reflected on the way I cook. My daughter, for instance, flew in from Colorado to help nurse me back to health. One day I asked her to pull out all the seasonings in the kitchen cabinet that contain salt. Mind you, a few days earlier I had just finished cooking Christmas dinner: baked chicken and the works. I didn't do a big turkey because I didn't feel well. Plus, I knew I had a surgical procedure coming up. But even though I scaled back on the bird, I had just about everything else on the menu. I made the best collard greens I'd ever made, but I made them with ham hocks. I made macaroni that was like to die for –- and I almost did. Sausage stuffing, yams, potato salad, ham –- all this food just for me and my wife.

When my daughter pulled out the seasonings I used to prepare that Christmas dinner, I discovered I had seven or eight "salts" in the cabinet. I have seasoning salt. I have seafood seasoning. I have garlic salt. I do have celery seed, but I used celery salt. I have onion powder but I used onion salt.

Tony Leaner

I must have put five to seven layers of salt on that chicken. I learned this from my family. We felt proud that no one needed the salt and pepper shakers or the hot sauce at our dinner table. That meant we had seasoned the food. But I can't cook like that anymore, so what do I do now? The first few meals I made after my surgery were so horrible, I almost went back to the salt.

My mom, who had high blood pressure, used to complain of the same thing. As an exceptional cook, she knew the natural seasonings she could use as a substitute, but even she would try to sneak in the salt. Unfortunately all that salt would cause her to retain fluid, and she would have to go to the doctor for diuretics and other treatments. Every three or four months, she'd go into the hospital for two or three days to get rid of all that fluid. She would be okay for a while, and then start the cycle all over again. That process continued for the last three or four years of her life.

I'm more focused on my family history. Diabetes runs in my family. In fact, family members have said that diabetes is more prevalent in the men than the women, and every other person gets it. My father had it; my older brother didn't get it. My sister didn't get it, but my younger brother has diabetes. I'm driven to speak out about this issue because I have four grandchildren: three boys and a daughter. They could end up with diabetes because of their genetic history.

My older brother died from emphysema due to years of smoking. I smoked when I was younger. When my dad finally quit after 40 years of smoking, he beat up everyone else about their smoking habits. Fortunately I heard what he had to say and I quit. My mom continued for a while, and my older brother stopped after doctors diagnosed his emphysema. But by then it was 10 years too late.

I did not share my personal and family history with my doctors. When I used to go to the doctor, I never really thought much about answering those questions about family medical history. I didn't realize that a doctor could use that information to identify patterns or keep an eye out for certain issues. Probably like most guys, those questions weren't important to me because I didn't understand the relevance. My answers to those questions were probably flighty and incomplete because I didn't take my family health history seriously.

Not only is my family history important, but my personal history also matters. As in the case of my Great-uncle Harold, what my doctor doesn't know can hurt me. He died of prostate cancer but never mentioned the signs like blood in his stool to his doctors. By the time he told his doctor it was too late. He died within a year of the diagnosis of his cancer.

Some of us do go to the doctor when we don't feel well. But other men get scared and run in the opposite direction. How many of us are carrying a secret we don't want to deal with? Addressing an issue sooner can help us heal faster, avoid more invasive procedures or recover more quickly.

Some of us respond with false bravado: "Hey, I'm going to die of something anyway. Why do I need to go to the doctor?" Hey, if that's you, more power to you. All I can tell you is that when the doctor says something is wrong, that's not how most people respond. We're afraid -- and we want help.

Tony Leaner

I have a new respect for diabetes. When I was in the hospital just before New Year's 2012, I thought I could still decide whether to have a stent or to have open heart surgery. I learned that because of my diabetes, stents were not an option. What's more, my diabetes made it harder for me to feel pain and realize something was wrong with my body. By sticking to my poor diet and health habits, I actually was helping my disease take me out.

While co-hosting my wife Deborah's TV show, "Ms. Deborah's Tearoom," I interviewed Dr. Vic Raya, a cardiologist with Capitol Cardiology who performs surgery at both Southern Maryland and Prince George's hospitals. Dr. Raya made the following statement: "Of all the silent killers, diabetes is like an assassin." That statement changed my life. I'd never heard anyone speak about diabetes that way. The lights went off. The alarm sounded. The dots finally connected.

The main job or function of diabetes is to go out much like a hired assassin and kill any organ in your body it can. Diabetes, for example, can kill nerves in your feet. That's why the most common cause of amputations in this country isn't Iraq or Afghanistan, according to Dr. Raya. The most common cause is diabetes.

Diabetes causes kidney failure, and the most common causes of dialysis are diabetes or hypertension. Diabetes can cause blindness. This disease also can deaden nerves in the heart so that, like me, a person suffering a heart attack might not even feel a pain that alerts him to go to the hospital. You could have a heart attack and never know.

Listening to Dr. Raya, I realized I had acted as an informant. I had been an accomplice to my diabetes. I was sharpening the knife and loading the bullets in the weapons of the very thing that was attempting to take me out of here. I was actually helping this assassin, released in my body by my lackluster lifestyle, to go about its business of killing me.

It's taken some time, but I've decided to make my health a priority. Even if my wife doesn't want to alter her diet or make changes to her exercise routine, I'm still responsible for my own health. We can't wait for our wives to begin cooking differently before we decide to do better. We have to change.

Tony Leaner

Chapter Three Assessment

o Do you eat starchy foods (rice, potatoes, bread) frequently?

o How often do you eat fried foods?

o Do you eat the extra large portion sizes?

o Do you eat high-sodium prepared foods often?

o Do you know your family health history?

o Have you discussed your family's health history with siblings and other relatives?

o Are you honest with your doctor about your personal health history? Have you shared all your issues and ailments with your physician?

o Do you fear going to the doctor?

Easy Fixes:

o Take your lunch to work one day this week and give yourself a break from the fast food restaurant or local carryout.

o Replace your usual soda with a bottle of water one day this week.

CHAPTER FOUR
The Power of the Pew

I coined the phrase "the power of the pew" after my arrest for my bad, inconsistent health habits. During my rehabilitation, I experienced this wonderful, built-in support system in the faith-based community. All I had to do was tap into it by investing in it. This support system also confirmed a life lesson my deceased father-in-law, Frank Fletcher, shared with me and my son Korey, who is now also deceased. Allow me to share it with you.

Back in the late 90s, my wife and I moved into an area of Prince George's County, Maryland, where we knew absolutely no one. I mean, not a soul. Shortly after relocating, some very dear friends of ours, the Taylors, invited us to attend the wedding of their daughter, which took place in the church that we would later join.

As a result of that wedding weekend, we visited and within six months joined First Baptist Church of Glenarden under the leadership of Pastor John K. Jenkins, Sr., in December 1999. Now remember, neither my wife nor I knew anyone in that church other than the Taylors, who invited us to the wedding. They had moved out of the area about three years before this wedding but had maintained relationships there. My wife and I, however, were on our own, so to speak. Nevertheless, we involved ourselves in ministry as we had done at our previous church. We served wherever God called us to serve and naturally progressed into leadership.

Almost 12 years later to the day, I suffered my heart attack and was airlifted to Washington Hospital Center for an emergency operation. I underwent a triple bypass operation five days later. I gave you all of that background to get to this point: Words cannot describe the outpouring of support my wife and I received from my church family, and it all came about as a direct result of the "power of the pew." The support, the love and the acts of kindness showered upon us flowed from our connection to the assembly in which we served.

I've Got Benefits

My father-in-law, Frank Fletcher, used to passionately talk about BENEFITS whenever he spoke to me and my son, his grandson, Korey. As the only man on that side of the family, Frank used to say those words with such meaning, authority and passion. My father-in-law, however, was a construction worker, a hardworking guy who liked to party a little too much. So although I heard about these benefits over and over again, I just thought he had a little too much "party" going on, if you know what I mean.

What I didn't know was that I was getting a lesson in wisdom. My father-in-law tried to school me and Korey on how to recognize these benefits through a different set of eyes. Years later I realized what my father-in-law was trying to say when I received some of those benefits, benefits available to me just because of my relationship with my brothers in Christ.

Who is this guy?

I was scheduled for an outpatient surgery at Johns Hopkins University Hospital in late December 2011, to remove a cancerous tumor off of my neck. A few of my brothers in Christ came and prayed with me at 5:30 a.m. before I went into surgery. While I was under the knife, my wife sat in the surgery waiting room with my spiritual sister, Josephine, as well as some of the ladies in Divine Discipleship for Sisters (DDS), a ministry she started in 2003.

At the surgeon's request, I stayed overnight after the surgery for observation to make sure things went well. I actually didn't feel well when my wife arrived to take me home the next day, but I was just glad to be leaving. I slept well that night, but the next day I just couldn't get myself together. Doctors usually tell you to expect some discomfort after surgery because of the anesthesia, but as the day went on I knew something was wrong.

My wife called Johns Hopkins and described what was happening to me. The doctor suggested that I get to the nearest hospital as soon as possible. James, one of my brothers in Christ, just happened to call to check on me at that time. When he heard that I needed to get to the hospital, he came over and helped me get dressed so my wife could take me to the nearest hospital. I was going downhill fast. I wasn't looking or feeling well, and I walked like a 90-year-old man as I moved from station to station in the hospital to undergo various tests in the emergency room.

Finally I received an EKG. When the doctor on call read the results, the emergency room staff sprang into action. It seemed as if 50 or more people seemingly came out of nowhere to start administering medicine. They started giving me meds in my mouth, sticking IV's in my arm and checking my vital signs. It felt surreal. Kinda like a circus.

So the doctor came in and said, "Sir, you are having a heart attack." I looked at him and said, "What?" I didn't feel any pain and I wasn't experiencing any of the symptoms associated with a heart attack. I learned later that my inability to feel pain stemmed from my diabetes. The joke on me was I had gone to Doctors Community Hospital that evening expecting to get a simple prescription and go home.

By this time my wife had walked out of the room to make some calls. The next thing I knew, Mike, a friend and member of the ministerial staff at our church, appeared by my bedside. He talked to me and kept me calm while the staff prepared to take me to Washington Hospital Center by helicopter. As God would have it, Mike was in the same emergency ward tending to his wife's grandmother.

When my wife got back to my room, Mike had already assessed the situation and was ready to give my wife a report as to what was happening to me. My wife had called her sisters and a few brothers in our circle to ask for prayer. The word got out and prayers went up to God for me from all over the United States and internationally.

I felt those prayers, and by the time I came out of emergency surgery -- where they put a stent in my right artery, which was 99 percent blocked -- the waiting room was full of people we knew. Many of them served within our church. It was about 1:30 a.m., and people were still coming to the hospital. The nurses decided to let the visitors see me 3 by 3, but at some point the nurses said stop, "No more, not another person."

In fact, when the nurses moved me to intensive care, they tried to hurry it up so that they wouldn't be surrounded by all the people hanging out in the waiting room. This is when I slightly began to understand what my father-in-law meant about those "benefits." I knew serving the Lord would pay off after while, as the song says. But I honestly didn't know or expect the love shown to me by my brothers and sisters in Christ during this season. This was over the top.

Man, I felt so much confidence knowing that prayers were going up for me. The brothers were by my bedside on every floor of that hospital. The nurses would say, "Who is this man?" Someone would reply, "My brother in Christ." I believe this is the type of benefit my father-in-law was trying to help my son and I understand. I didn't realize how dynamic this concept was until I became entrenched in what I call "the power of the pew."

The Power Source

The power source that fuels these types of relationships, this type of brotherly love, is Jesus Christ. This level of care is unbelievable to those who aren't aware of the power source. The morning of my third surgery, the triple bypass, the brothers in Christ were back once again at 5:30 in the a.m.

praying for my open heart surgery. Thank you, Jesus, for their prayers because the surgeon told me and my wife afterward that my heart stopped twice during the surgery. God used the power of the pew to heal me! In fact, the night before the surgery, after all the visitors left around 1:30 a.m., I couldn't go to sleep and my pressure was rising. If it continued to rise, I couldn't have the surgery. That thought stressed me out even more.

But thanks to my brothers and sisters in Christ, I now understood that prayer was the navigator for my success. So I called my wife and asked her to let the saints know what was going on. She asked my head prayer warrior, Mrs. Lucille, to call and pray with me. I went to sleep with the prayers of the righteous hovering over me that night. When I awoke the next morning, my blood pressure was down and the hospital staff prepped me for surgery. Man, the prayers of the righteous avail much.

Before I even came home from the hospital, many of the brothers had already talked to my wife to make sure that my household wouldn't want for anything. One brother paid my mortgage so that I wouldn't have to worry while healing. Another came over and checked the furnace to ensure that nothing went wrong. Many brothers brought food and firewood so I could sit in front of the fireplace and heal. The DDS women organized a system to ensure that we had breakfast, lunch and dinner for more than a three-week period. They brought so much food, we had to ask them to stop.

Other people came by and prayed. Many just quietly put money in my hand or my wife's hand for incidentals.

When my wife had to go out, brothers came and sat with me. One brother came back during the spring and power washed and stained the deck so I could relax outdoors during the warmer weather. I can't begin to share all the love we received from my pastor, the ministers, the deacons and deaconess and the church at large. In addition, my neighbors prayed, brought food, sent fruit baskets and the like.

Foundational Thinking

I coined the phrase "power of the pew" based on some foundational thinking I discovered in Hebrews 10:24-25, a biblical scripture that urges us to fellowship with one another within the assembly of the congregation. Indeed, Hebrews 10:24 says, "Let us consider one another." This means fellowship with God must never become selfish.

The verses continue: "And let us consider one another to provoke unto love and good works; [25] not forsaking our own assembling together, as the custom of some is, but exhorting one another; and so much the more, as ye see the day drawing nigh "

God calls us to fellowship with other Christians in a local assembly. Apparently the writer's observation was that some believers had been wavering in their thinking and keeping themselves away from church. It's interesting to note that the emphasis isn't on what a believer gets from the assembly, but rather on what he can contribute to the assembly. Faithfulness in church attendance encourages others and provokes them to love and good works. It's about making an investment in others. You don't do it looking for a return, but you know the return will show up just when you need it.

I think my First Lady, Trina Jenkins, put it best when she said to my wife, "All that happened to you both was that God allowed you to receive back the same love that you both have given to the ministry." There really is power in the pew! There's a residue that comes off of what you invest in the assembly –- a return on investment that can't be compared to anything on Wall Street. You know the saying: You can't beat God giving. Well, I'm here to declare you can't. No matter how much you try you can't even come close.

But it all stems from not only being part of the assembly but working in that assembly. So many of us as men just do church. Come on now; don't look at me in that tone of voice. You know I'm telling the truth. We go to church; we take our families to church. We might even get to Bible study. But I'm challenging us all, myself included, to pursue another dimension of involvement.

We have to go deeper in our pursuit of our relationship with God. We have to make a concerted effort to pull the mask off and stop hiding behind what somebody did or didn't do for us or to us. As men we have to dive in and get wet. As a friend of mine, Dr. Johnny Parker, says, we have to stop water skiing, put on the equipment and go deep-sea diving. Not snorkeling but diving.

We have to allow relationships to develop. I know this is difficult because it's not natural for us as men to allow this type of closeness to develop. I think you have to be a man to understand how we think, but our natural tendency is not to share. We hold things very close to the vest, so to speak. We are for the most part very private with our stuff, and I'm convinced that's part of what contributes to our poor performance when it comes to interacting with our doctors. We as men don't know how to share our fears or inner thoughts, especially if those thoughts pertain to insecurities. We look at that as being weak or soft, so we're hard pressed to open up ourselves that way. But the benefits I'm talking about come out of this arena when we push past fear and pride, step out on faith and groom Godly relationships with other men so we can get free from the imprisonment of that thinking. Once that happens, we tap into the benefits of the assembly, the power of the pew.

My father-in-law would say, "You got benefits," but you can't buy them or pay for them. They come from the power source Himself. Your position on the leadership ladder isn't important. It can happen to you on any level. You just need some involvement in ministry to give "the power in the pew" some traction.

These benefits are free when we get in real relationship with God and operate with and through His people. Try it. I promise you it works.

Tony Leaner

Chapter Four Assessment

o Are you a member of a local church?

o Are you involved in a ministry in that church?

o Do you have relationships with brothers in Christ?

o What are the concerns that keep you from wanting to make a deeper commitment to your church? (For example, negative things you saw in church as a child; lack of integrity among church leaders; etc.)

CHAPTER FIVE
If There is Anything I Can Do, Seriously...

A few weeks into my recovery, the brothers started coming over as time would allow to sit and talk with me. I'd have breakfast, take a shower, get dressed and then come down to my family room. My wife would light a fire in the fireplace that would last all day. Those winter mornings by the fire were so relaxing and therapeutic for me as I talked to my friends and reflected on my life's journey.

These guys decided to coordinate among themselves and bring firewood to my home two to three times per week as needed. They didn't ask permission. We didn't have a conversation about it. They just saw the apparent need and filled it.

In February, during one of these visits, a guy looked out back and observed that my deck needed power washing. He knew that I couldn't do it, and he happened to do that kind of work as a side business to his regular job. When the weather broke he came by and power washed the deck. He later returned and re-stained it. He saw a task he could do, so he stepped right in and took care of it.

Tony Leaner

You can always find a way to render help or provide a service to someone who's recovering from a major illness or reeling from a significant loss. And like the guys who brought firewood to my house and power washed my deck, you don't have to wait for a direct, specific request.

One of the craziest things I heard during my illness came from someone who said, "Let me know if there's anything you need." I know this person sincerely meant well. No doubt he wanted me to know that if I needed something and made a simple phone call, he would be "Johnny on the Spot" and meet that need post haste.

But if we really thought about our words, we'd ask the question differently. Here's a slightly different slant on how we can offer ourselves and take the burden and maybe even the guilt away from the person in need.

Standing in the Gap

First of all, there's always going to be a need. Large or small, there's always going to be something you can do in a time of crisis. So the first thing I want to do is remove the word "IF." It's not if but what and how you and I can fill that void. A better solution would be to turn the question back to ourselves and ask: "What do I need to do here? How can I meet the obvious need in this situation?"

I often think about something my father said years ago when discussing entrepreneurship. If you want to start a successful business, he said, find a void and fill it. Amazingly, we often overlook this simple concept when it comes to helping people. Instead of asking, "Is there anything I can do," or "What do you need," just look for the void in the person's situation and fill it.

Here in Maryland, for example, we recently experienced several bad storms. The storms brought down trees and power lines and left countless people, including myself, without power for days. Nevertheless, people came together to help each other. Neighbors and friends came by the house and began taking inventory of the void. No fanfare. No big process. They just identified the need or void and began to fill it.

Imagine that you're sitting in a house with no electricity and you hear a knock on the door. There on your doorstep is a neighbor with food and an extension cord plugged into their gas generator. He tells you to plug your refrigerator and a lamp into the extension cord so you can get by until the power company restores electricity. Wow, what a wonderful thought.

We can have the same impact when someone we know experiences a life event and needs our help. If you're a good cook, prepare several meals. Some of us are great with our hands. I'm not, but I know guys who have gifts in that area. So take inventory. Can you fix something around the house? Maybe the house needs a wheelchair ramp to accommodate a recent health challenge. One guy who had a triple bypass like I did said his neighbors cut his lawn for him during his recovery period.

Or perhaps the gutters need cleaning. Two of my friends, Carlton and Darryl, came over one Saturday and handled mine. A crew of guys came over the day that I was released from the hospital to move some furniture and TV's around so I would feel more comfortable when I got home. I thank that whole crew because a bunch of guys showed up, and you know who you are. Several other brothers stood ready to take me to doctor's appointments or help me run errands. And one guy came over and just sat with me while my wife went out for several hours to take care of some business she needed to get done.

There's always something you can do, so don't wait for someone to ask or give directions. Step right up and volunteer. A person might not need your money – and I'm not discounting the importance of money. Your time and effort, however, could prove even more valuable. In any case, find the void or need and fill it. You'll bless someone's life – and you'll get a blessing as well!

CHAPTER SIX
We Are Family

Sickness or tragedy can draw a family unit together--or drive a wedge into an already shaky relationship.

My brother-in-law and I, for example, had drifted apart over the years. I don't know how it happened, but we really developed a disdain for each other. When I took ill and my surgery was eminent, my sister wanted to be present and, in the eleventh hour, he volunteered to make the drive with her. He and I got a chance to speak a few times and resolved our differences. We've enjoyed a rebirth of what had always been an enjoyable relationship.

Don't wait until sickness strikes to get things right with your friends and loved ones. Some families are small, and it seems like we have family dying all the time. No one's perfect, and every family has some dysfunction. But I encourage you to work through those issues now so you don't have to attend a funeral burdened with guilt and unresolved issues.

No one wins when relatives stop caring and speaking to one another. Watching family members treat each other with indifference is painful, even to outsiders. Case in point: After my emergency stent surgery on the 29th of December,

Tony Leaner

I stayed in intensive care for observation. After about thirty hours, the hospital staff moved me to pre-op because it was the New Year's weekend pending my triple bypass operation, which was to take place on January 3rd.

They moved me into my new room late in the evening, around 11:00. Another patient, "Clarence," was in the room already. Clarence had been there for about a week for an extensive stent operation, and the hospital planned to release him the next morning.

But Clarence kept telling the medical staff he wasn't ready. He had no one at home to care for him, and he wasn't comfortable going home alone. He had no one with whom he could stay. All of his family lived outside the District of Columbia, and although he had informed them the day before of his release, no one had time to come transport him. When the nurses asked how he had arrived at the hospital, Clarence said a neighbor had brought him; however, that neighbor had charged him $25 to bring him to the emergency room.

As his roommate, I couldn't help overhearing all of this. I started making calls and found someone to transport Clarence, but at the last minute one of his relatives came to get him. This relative complained the entire time about having to help Clarence.

We should make up our minds to be better than this. We are our brother's keeper. I pray that there's nothing in my relationships with family or friends that would cause me to turn a cold shoulder toward someone in that kind of need. We can't allow anger, malice, unforgiveness and selfishness to dictate our response to someone in need let alone a relative.

I'm so thankful for the family and friends God has

given me. We have our issues and faults, but when push comes to shove we're there for each other. My sister and her husband came across country from the Midwest to be by my side. My brother was on the phone getting a play-by-play account of my procedures. My cousin came in from New York and one of my daughters flew in from Colorado. That's not counting the 30 people who rallied around my wife during my emergency operation.

In fact, I had more than 200 visitors during my 10-day stay at Washington Hospital Center. They know who they are, and I'm grateful to God that they cared enough about me to be there in my time of need. I also want to thank my pastor, Pastor John K. Jenkins, and his wife Trina for showing me so much love during this season of my life.

CHAPTER SEVEN
My Lady and Myself

During the years prior to my heart attack, my wife often tried to help me change my eating habits or take better care of myself as a person with diabetes.

When we'd go out to eat, I'd typically order my favorite meal of fried chicken, French fries and sweetened iced tea. I'd have three or four free refills of iced tea while we ate and leave the restaurant with another cup of that stuff in my hand.

"Honey, do you think you should eat that?" my wife would say. Other times she'd ask, "Are you sure you're okay? Is it time for that doctor's appointment?"

I'd assure my wife that I had everything under control. Truthfully, I was out of control, but I didn't want to listen to her words of caution. So I turned a deaf ear and kept on eating and behaving as I always had.

My outlook on my health and my marriage has changed since my heart attack. My illness highlighted the vows we made June 18, 1983, vows that of course included the words, "in sickness and in health, 'til death do us part." My illness also brought to light how much I had taken not only this vow but also my wife for granted during 29 years of marriage.

Sure, I can say unequivocally that I knew 29 years ago that Deborah was in it for the long haul. I'd certainly given her many reasons and opportunities to "bail out" of our marriage prior to getting sick. So I know that wasn't even an option.

Around 2007, in fact, after a teaching series by our pastor on the marriage covenant, I recommitted myself to my wife by reconfirming that divorce would never be an option for our union. Even so, nothing truly prepares a spouse for the role of caregiver.

Did I Say 'I Do' To This?!

Caregiving is a thankless job, but if you've ever been ill you have a special appreciation for those who played this role in your life. Without them, some of us wouldn't have made it through.

During my first week home after my heart attack, I decided I wanted to take a long hot shower. I couldn't do it -- at least not on my own! Doctors had opened up my chest to do the surgery, and I had limited motor skills. I couldn't lift anything weighted, and I couldn't raise my hands beyond my shoulder blades.

So my wife had to bathe me every morning and help me get dressed. Deborah had to change bandages and apply new ointments to my surgical wounds. In fact, she had to clean my wounds. She was Nurse Deborah; she didn't have the credentials, but as my wife she was willing to do whatever she had to do.

I remember for the first week I couldn't sleep in my bed. I had to sleep in my recliner, every time I laid down it was as if my airways were closing down. All night my wife would have to wake up to let the recliner down so I could go to the restroom. She would then give me my medications, help me back into my recliner, cover me up and get me back to sleep -- only to have to repeat this two or three more times during the night.

Other wives in similar circumstances found they had to set their schedules and interests aside to be there for their husbands physically, emotionally and spiritually. That could mean everything from driving their husbands to appointments to cutting tape for bandages. Their husbands were fighting for life, and this wasn't the time to break down in tears. No, they had to be strong for their men. As my wife says, the household changes when this kind of crisis shows up on your doorstep.

Is this what we signed up for when we said our vows? You bet, but nobody gives it a second thought until we have to walk out that vow in real life. Nothing can prepare anyone for that walk.

Man Enough to Accept Help

I've seen some common threads as I talk to my friends about their illnesses. I've noticed, for example, how these men struggled to accept help from others, including their spouses.

One friend told me how he had to rush back to the hospital three days after going home, all because he decided he could move from his bedroom to the bathroom without any assistance. He fell and reopened his surgical wounds.

Another friend said he went downstairs to the main floor of his home from his bedroom after his wife left to run errands. He soon found that he didn't have the strength to get back upstairs. He had to sit on the steps and wait until his wife returned an hour later so she could help him back to the bedroom.

I too remember that drive to progress quickly to the next level of healing. My doctors cautioned me not to rush things and move too fast. I'm telling you this now so that when your wife tells you the same thing, you won't perceive her advice as nagging. Come on, now, "Tell the truth and shame the devil," as the seasoned folk say.

Tested by Illness

In light of all we've experienced with my health, my wife and I feel closer as a couple. We've become wiser together. Our love is deeper, much richer and fuller than before, and our future is more pronounced and focused. We don't even have intense fellowship (argue) like we did before. In fact, some things just don't have the same importance when it comes to who's right or wrong.

You don't measure the success of your marriage by how you celebrate the good times. The real test is in how you support each other through challenges. My wife and I went through a tsunami – and if we made it, you can too. All of our marriages, however, have a better chance of surviving these storms if we invest in the vows we made ahead of time. Don't sit and wait until the test comes. Take time to prepare and study for the test that's on its way to your house. Here are a few of the lessons I learned:

1. Learn to be a true friend. True friendship is like God's grace; it's giving unmerited favor to someone and seeking to comfort, help and meet someone else's need, not your own. Proverbs 18:24 says, "A man that hath friends must show himself friendly." In other words, we have to work on building our friendship as husband and wives. Sometimes we can hear what's best for us from everyone but our spouse. In fact, we sometime suspect her words because we think our spouse has selfish motives. It's a trick of the enemy. Trust that what's best for the marriage will ensure that you both will win.

We also can get caught up in who's doing more for the kids, house, relationship and so on. Marriage isn't about that. Friendship isn't one-sided. It's based on giving, not getting. If you invest in your friendship as a couple, you'll get a return that money can't buy. That investment will pay off when that storm shows up at your house.

You'll get another kind of payoff if you don't invest in your friendship. Adversity hits twice as hard in those relationships where the husband and wife haven't used this principle. Storms can open up old wounds and heighten uncertainty and insecurity. They can cause self-esteem to plummet and drive a wedge in what's already a struggling relationship.

Remember my roommate Clarence? My sense is that at least part of the problem was Clarence. Not being judgmental; just stating an observation. Clarence seemed to be set in his ways. He wasn't a bad guy, but you couldn't tell him anything. It appeared to me that he hadn't spent a lot of time or resources in developing, maintaining or nurturing loving, fruitful relationships. In other words, Clarence had stopped putting deposits in the relationship bank accounts with family and friends. When Clarence needed to make a withdrawal from his account, he had no balance and may have even been overdrawn.

Sounds like anybody you know? I don't want to be like that, so I have to take an introspective review of myself and my baggage regularly. Taking a hard look at yourself isn't easy and it definitely doesn't feel good. I'm not suggesting that we as guys are all at fault. No, what I'm saying is this is low-hanging fruit. Taking just a little time to assess yourself can pay off big later. I hope you never have to make this kind of withdrawal from someone's emotional bank account. But know this: The wrong time to be working on your relationship bank with your ultimate caregiver is after you've fallen ill and need that person's support.

2. Remember love is an act of the will. Love isn't just a romantic feeling. It's a commitment of the will to the true good of each other. You didn't promise your wife a feeling when you took your vows. Love is a commitment of choice. What does intimacy have to do with it? For starters, when trouble comes into a marriage, the first thing that seems to go out the window is intimacy/sex. In every other biological function, such as eating, growing, and so on, the man and woman are separate organisms. However, when the two become one flesh and the union functions in harmony -- and I'm not just talking about our bodies -- I mean experience harmony at every level. When we as husband and wife complete each other in sexual self-giving, the hearts and minds and spirits of the husband and wife cooperate with their bodies and they're unified not just in body but in every dimension in life.

In other words, if you invest in your friendship you can walk out your challenges together as one.

Now right about here I can sense in my spirit that if you're a man reading this chapter, you might be ready to dive out of this chapter or out of this book altogether. I beg you to hang tough. What's often good or best for me doesn't always feel or sound good. If something doesn't please our senses, we as men often prefer to dismiss the whole thing and not deal with it.

The purpose of this advice is to get you a "Get Out of Jail" card. If you apply just some of these things, I promise you'll enjoy good success in your relationships and in your health.

My friend, Van, who was in a coma for 30 days, applauds the care and dedication shown by his wife during his long battle with complications from swine flu.

"When I go back to the hospital to visit the staff, they all say they don't remember me, but they remember that my wife was at the hospital all the time," says Van. "She was there every day like clockwork." My wife and I are much closer after that experience. Many people have said I wouldn't be alive if not for God and my wife.

Tony Leaner

Tony & Deborah Leaner

ARRESTED: From Bad Habits to Breakthrough

Interviews with Some Ex-Offenders

When you're serving time in jail, you usually end up with cell mates. These guys aren't necessarily friends that you knew previously -- although a very good friend of mine who's an ex-offender once told me that in his case, several of his friends ended up in the same prison at the same time. That's because they were all about doing crime, maybe even the same crime, so they got sentenced together.

Like my ex-offender friend, some of us like to hang out with others while we're indulging in bad habits. We might eat all the wrong foods at the tailgate party every weekend or drink too much during that fishing trip. On the other hand, some guys are white-collar criminals; they work too hard and carry too much stress. In either case, there's a price to pay.

I've asked some fellow inmates to share with you the stories behind their arrests for poor health. On the following pages, they'll reveal the health crimes they committed and how their lifestyle choices nearly sentenced them to death. These gentlemen served their time, experienced rehabilitation, and now enjoy healthy lives. But before they saw the error of their ways, they were, as I was, ARRESTED!

ARRESTED: From Bad Habits to Breakthrough

David Dawson Interview

My first heart attack was in March 1994, while I was living in Newark, New Jersey. My chest started hurting so bad, I laid on the floor. I thought I felt the pain in the middle of my back, so I asked my 8-year-old daughter to walk on my back, which she really enjoyed. The pain seemed to go away. I thought maybe it was indigestion, like I had to burp.

The next day I went to work and they told me I was put on the night shift, which I hated. So I went back home and went back that night. I felt the same pain. That time I thought it was because I didn't get enough sleep. Come to find out, I'd had another heart attack.

Two weeks later I had the big one. By the grace of God my stepson came by the house to borrow something, and he looked at me and said, "Wow, Dad, you look gray." He'd never seen me look like that before. I was in so much pain I didn't know what to do. Sweat was rolling off of me. He just picked me up, threw me over his back and put me in his car.

He called my wife and told her something was wrong with me. I felt like nothing was wrong. In fact, I lit a cigarette while I was in the car. My stepson pulled the cigarette out of my mouth and threw it out the car window. That was the last cigarette I smoked.

When I got to the hospital, four doctors were there waiting for me. They told me I was having a heart attack. I felt better after they gave me morphine, so I thought I could go home. They said, "Oh, no, you're not." They said I was still having a heart attack. I was in United Hospitals Medical

Tony Leaner

Center for four days, and then spent 10 days in Beth Israel Hospital Center.

The Power of Prayer

I recovered from the heart attacks, and over the years I was fine up until 2005. Then I had a stroke that left me paralyzed on my left side for two years. I think that came from neglecting my health -- not going to doctors the way I should have, especially because I also had high blood pressure. Doctors at the Veteran's Administration hospital have also said my heart attacks and stroke came from being exposed to Agent Orange in Vietnam.

In 2006, I started suffering from a sore throat. I went to the doctors, and they said I had throat cancer. Here I am in a wheelchair. I'm going to the doctor, and they're telling me I have cancer in my throat. So I went to my niece, who's an evangelist, and I asked her to call the prayer warriors together. They laid me on the floor, held my niece over my body, and they prayed for me. I felt that I was healed.

The doctor said I had to come back the following Friday at 6 a.m. for radiation treatment. I got there at 7:30. When they asked why I didn't show up, I said I had no reason to. I told them they weren't going to do anything to me until they took more X-rays. The second X-ray showed no cancer.

One night while I was in the wheelchair, I said, you know, I'm going to get up tomorrow and go to the bathroom by myself. You simply can't imagine what life is like without the use of your left hand. You can't button a shirt sleeve. You can't tie your tie. You can't even tie your shoes.

It's easy to see people in that condition, but to be in that condition is something else. And I just knew it would be temporary. You know you can make your leg move. You try with all your power. Your brain is telling your leg to move, and it won't move. But after I prayed that prayer that night, I was in the bathroom the next morning looking at myself in the mirror. My mouth was on the side of my face. My eye had pulled down on the side of my face – that's how disfigured I was. But there I was standing and looking at myself in the mirror.

Macho Man?

We as men, you know, we've got a lot of pride. We don't want to go to the doctor. We feel like we know everything, when we don't. It's just like a man going through the exam for prostate cancer. Some guys don't want to do the exam because they don't think it's manly. I didn't want a colonoscopy for the same reasons, but this is the only body we get to use on this earth.

My father died when I was 8, and I didn't have a father figure in my life to tell me how to take care of a man's body. My father was in the military, but I don't know how he died. As a young man, I didn't know if anyone in my family had problems with heart disease, high blood pressure or diabetes. Today I have a sister who's a diabetic. Fortunately, no one has died from a heart attack.

I got out of the military when I was 25 after eight years of service. I never went to the doctor for little things. I would rely on old remedies or just say, "Oh, I'm all right." I never went for a physical or a thorough check-up.

I didn't find out I was a diabetic until I went to Beth Israel to visit a friend of mine. People were conducting diabetes screenings in the hallways. They checked my fingers and said, "Oh, you're on the borderline. You need to have this checked." But I prolonged that too. I said, "I'm all right," because I felt all right – until one day I almost passed out in the grocery store. My sugar went down, and I was ready to pass out. I was trembling inside. A lady passed by me, then she came back with some orange juice and said, "Here, drink this. When you feel better, pay for it on the way out." I drank the juice and felt better right away.

I didn't go to the doctor because of that need to feel macho. Plus, I was always working. I was afraid that I would miss a day of work. I worked two and three jobs trying to make all the money I could make. I realize now that's not what life is about. But at that time it was just working, working, working, trying to take care of my home.

Is There a Nurse in the House?

My first wife, interestingly enough, was a nurse. But most of the time I would leave early in the morning and come back late at night. She tried to get me to go to the doctor, and after that heart attack I did go in for exams a little more, but not as much as I should have.

My second wife took care of me after the stroke. I was so independent that I would slide down the steps to go outside. Still, she had to help me get up to go to the bathroom. Having a woman try to lift a man is something else. She could only hold me on my left side, and I would use my right side, my stronger side, to keep her from falling also.

She had to make sure I was dressed properly. My stroke affected my left side, and I couldn't really squeeze a washcloth with one hand. But I would wet the cloth and use my right had to wash my left side. But I couldn't use my left hand to wash my right side, so I depended on her to do that.

I'd get in the shower and just stand on my right side. Then a guy put a chair in my shower. But I was determined I would do better. I wasn't going to stay that way forever. I felt helpless at times, but I knew this was a part-time situation.

I always tried to do things to make myself stronger. I would stand up and she would say, "Sit down." But when you sit all the time, you don't want to sit.

I went to therapy six days a week at the VA hospital in East Orange. I would hold on to the rail and walk sideways to the left to build my left leg back up. It hurt, probably because I would fall a lot. In certain parts of my leg I had no feeling at all. I couldn't feel my left hand because it was twisted.

Fighting the Negative with Positive

During this time I received disability from the VA and social security disability also. Sitting home all day, hearing other people go to work, was the worst thing in the world. I was very depressed; matter of fact, the VA had me on some medication, but I began to feel like I couldn't sleep without it. So I got off that medication.

A friend of mine, Alexander Brown, helped me get over the depression. I had met him in Panama when I was

Tony Leaner

17 years old and in the military. We reconnected at the VA in 2004. He would come by and take me out to the park or to a restaurant. He would hold my right side and try to get me to use my left side. He took me to physical therapy when my wife had to work.

He gave me positive encouragement. I would give negative things out to him and he would give positive back. Plus he gave me outings to anticipate. He would call and say, "How are you doing today?" I'd say, "Down and out." He'd say, "Don't worry; I'll be there in a little while."

People I thought were my friends didn't want anything to do with me because I couldn't walk. They were associates – they only wanted to be around you to ride in your car when they didn't have one. Alexander was my best friend. He was always there.

Full Recovery

I'm recovered except for the two fingers on my left hand that are still numb. I get out and run around the track. When I first started walking again, I had to use a cane or a walker because my left leg was smaller from nonuse. I fell a lot, but I got out and walked every day.

I would still go to physical therapy and walk, walk, walk. I would lift my legs with the weights. I just did what I had to do, and God blessed me to stand up.

When I could walk again, I realized I needed to take care of myself. The body is like a car: You've got to take it to the shop sometimes. And I wasn't doing that with my body. Since my health has been restored, I've walked six to six and a half miles a day because I can. God is good.

Today I take much better care of myself. I get up in the morning and eat oatmeal. I eat a lot more salads, and I cut out sweets. I've lost nine pounds in the last three months due to walking and watching what I eat.

Today, when I see people walking slowly around the track with a cane, I slow down and walk with them. I told one guy about my past. He started crying, and then he said, "If you can do it, I can do it." In two weeks' time, this man was able to walk without his cane. A lady on the track, who was also from the New York area, would walk slowly, really dragging, because of a stroke. I told her, "You can do it. Every little bit you put in, you get a lot out." She's walking around the track two and three times now.

In the Huddle

I'm involved with the men's group, the Huddle, at my church, but I talk to men about my experiences one on one. It's good to have God in our lives, but He gives us wisdom and knowledge too. I tell other men we have to take care of this vessel.

The younger people look at you as though you're old, but if they keep living, they'll be this age one day. My grandson tells me now, "Wow, grandpa, I can't run as long as you. You walk fast." But at one time I couldn't walk, so now I understand what it is to walk. I took it for granted. I thought I could just get up tomorrow and do this and that, until it hits you that you can't do anything. Good health is a blessing.

Tony Leaner

Grab Hold of the Truth

When I tell younger guys about my story, 50 percent of them say, yeah, I'm going to do something. The other half blow it off. I can't force anybody to go to the doctor. I just feed them a little bit of information at a time and hope they grab hold to it. There are guys out there who are consumed with their work, and they're overweight and huffing and puffing when they walk up three stairs. I can tell them it's time to do something about their health. But the final decision is theirs.

ARRESTED: From Bad Habits to Breakthrough

Richard Melton Interview

Back in 2011 I started to have stomach pains. I'd been experiencing pain for quite some time, and at one point doctors had attributed it to ulcers. It wasn't supposed to be serious. But I continued to have stomach pains, and at times my stomach would just ache – it seemed like it had a hole in it - the pains were so sharp; but then it would subside.

In November 2011 the pain was so excruciating that my wife was about to call the ambulance. Instead, I just took myself to the emergency room. The medical staff said I probably had stomach poison or some type of food poisoning, and they gave me an antibiotic. About a week later, my stomach was still bothering me a little bit, but then it subsided.

I talked to my primary care physician in December and told her my concerns. She worried that my problem might be more than what the emergency room noted, so I had a colonoscopy right after Christmas. They found that I had diverticulosis, a condition that causes "pockets" to build up in your intestinal walls. These pockets can get infected at times and cause a stomachache. About 60 percent of people over 40 have it.

You can go along with diverticulosis with no other outbreaks or concerns for the rest of your life. But often people will have a stomachache, and they'll go to the doctor for an antibiotic and the stomachache will go away. Well, that doesn't address the root cause, those pockets in your intestinal walls. If they aren't flushed out, those pockets build up in your bowels, and they can get infected and rupture.

Tony Leaner

When the pockets burst or rupture, you now have diverticulitis. The body can become toxic, and you can die.

That's what happened to me.

Emergency Surgery

I had a colonoscopy, and the doctor told me I had diverticulosis. It wasn't supposed to be serious. I just needed to monitor it. I was due back in two weeks for a follow-up visit, but I never made it back because my colon ruptured.

The pain was unbearable. I was in Baltimore at the time, and I was close to the University of Maryland Hospital, so my wife told me to just go there. I wanted to come home to Upper Marlboro. I thought maybe if I took some Pepto-Bismol or something I would be fine. It was nothing but a stomachache – I guess I wanted to be macho. But I was on the road, and I almost had to pull over so she could call an ambulance to come get me. But I was close enough to the hospital that I made it there.

The emergency room staff started asking me questions, but the pain was just so bad, the more questions people asked me, the more doctors they brought in. Finally they took me back and did a CAT scan. That's when they determined that my colon had ruptured.

They did immediate surgery to cut out that part of my intestinal wall. In doing so, they had to place a colostomy bag on me for my bowels. So I was home with the bag on for approximately three months.

ARRESTED: From Bad Habits to Breakthrough

An Eye-opening Experience

During that time I went over in my mind what I had done wrong because I was a pretty healthy person. I worked out every day. I didn't drink or smoke. I thought I was fine, but a lot of us live with that fallacy that just because we're supposedly healthy, nothing is really wrong.

At any given time something can happen. But I do think my condition was attributed to fiber. That's all the doctor kept telling me: I needed to eat more fiber. And now that's definitely in my diet. It wasn't a hereditary thing, and even though I thought I ate pretty well, I guess I wasn't eating enough fiber.

Doctors also say that certain things like popcorn kernels can get lodged in your intestine. The pockets can also become weak and strained over time, years and years. Sooner or later they can burst, and once they rupture, your body can become toxic, and that can kill you. I even wonder if the colonoscopy I had in December might have punctured the intestinal wall, but I have no way to prove that. But I'd had stomach problems for a while. I'd had a colonoscopy in 2009 and 2010 but they never attributed it to anything. It wasn't until December 2011 that a medical professional finally told me I had diverticulosis.

This whole experience was just an eye-opener for me. I heard about someone who died of the same thing I had about 10 days later. That lady went into the hospital but she didn't come out. That made me realize the seriousness of my experience.

Tony Leaner

"Be a Man About It"

If I had tried to drive home like I wanted to do, I probably would have passed out on the side of the road. My body would have shut down from all the toxins. I was trying to tough it out because I grew up in a house with a lot of sisters. When I complained about a scratch or my knee hurting, they told me to be a man about it. Stop acting like a little girl.

From that point on, when things happened, I figured I had to be a man. I've got to take this. A man handles things, and if you're hurt, so what? Suck it up. That was my mindset.

So as a man, you think, I'm not going to the hospital. That would be weak. I'm going to be okay. Doctors can't do anything.

My wife persisted in getting me checked out because she'll go to the doctor for anything. In fact, she had me go back to my primary care physician after I went to the emergency room in November 2011. She said, "Richard, something just isn't right. We have to address this."

My Better Half

This ordeal made me appreciate my daughter and my wife so much more. Not that I didn't before, but this was definitely a close call for me.

I had the bag on for three months, and then the surgeon had to go back in and reverse the procedure. It was very humbling to live with a bag. I thank God that I didn't have to live with it for a lifetime because there are people who do need it for the rest of their lives. Fortunately I had a reversible procedure, so that made it somewhat easier on me, but it is definitely a humbling experience.

When I first came home from the hospital, my wife had to take care of my wounds because I was cut in two different places. I also was so heavily medicated that she had to change my bag. My bag had to be changed every day, and I wasn't able to do it, so she had to take care of that. I needed about two weeks to recover from surgery.

My 9-year-old daughter was so concerned because she'd never seen daddy breaking down or hurting. When the pains started getting severe in November, I was in tears on my knees, but when I got the antibiotics from the emergency room, I was okay. But that was just a fallacy. The problem still persisted.

Advocate for Your Health

Today, at age 47, I'm fine. I just try to maintain a good diet with salads and fiber. I didn't eat terribly before, but over time as you age, you need to flush your system. The one thing I tell people is eat your fiber and flush yourself. You never want to go through anything like I experienced. It was just so painful. I encourage people to get colonoscopies as well as CAT scans so doctors can look at the colon from all angles.

For people who have stomach pains, I'd tell them not to focus just on ulcers because they could have what I had. Some people say, "It's stress. That's the only reason why my stomach is hurting." Let a doctor examine you, because you definitely don't want to get in a position where that operation isn't reversible. You don't want to end up with a bag for the rest of your life.

People also should realize that they're their best doctors. Sometimes medical professionals will treat you like another number. They want to get you in and out, so they throw possible solutions at you; you're probably suffering from this, you probably have that. You're just another person to them.

You have to be your own doctor. You should request certain treatments and make sure doctors aren't just telling you what you want to hear. When I went to the emergency room in November 2011, the medical technicians should have diagnosed something more than food poisoning or stomach poison. I think they missed the boat. But they missed the boat because I wasn't persistent enough. I just listened and said, okay.

Ask questions. It's your body, and nobody knows your body better than you. Make sure these doctors know what you're experiencing, and don't accept these boilerplate answers as doctrine. The doctor is there to assist you, not to just get you in and out.

My primary care physician, for example, was so thorough and concerned. My ailment just didn't make sense to her. Once I didn't make it back for the follow-up after the colonoscopy, she handled me with kid gloves all the way through my experience. I applaud her for her patience and concern.

ARRESTED: From Bad Habits to Breakthrough

If This Could Happen to Him …

Guys, the ones who know me, have been receptive to my story because they know that I was in decent shape before this happened. Brothers went in for exams after my experience, and they got clean bills of health, but at least they went. They didn't want this to happen to them. I even encourage women to tell their husbands. Although I had that outbreak, it can always happen again, and it can happen to anyone.

ARRESTED: From Bad Habits to Breakthrough

Vincent McKenzie Interview

I had my stroke on November 11, 2000, my wife's birthday. It was a bright sunny day, and I remember fixing my wife some fried fish.

I had to go pick up my daughter from tennis practice at Prince George's Community College. I left the house at 10:00 a.m., and as I was making this left turn to get to the community college, something happened. I couldn't put any weight on my right side. I realized at that moment that I was having a stroke. I'm a doctor, a psychologist, and stroke is something I'm familiar with. And I knew it right away. With all my right side gone, I figured that I was probably having a stroke.

I was in the car, and as I sat there trying to make a left turn, all the drivers started blowing their horns at me. I thought, I wish they would come see what's wrong with me so I could get some help. But nobody came. So I sat there for a while, and then I realized that I had to get my daughter or the tennis instructors might leave her there by herself.

So I moved my right leg off the pedal and put my left leg on the pedal. And I managed to drive from there down to the tennis courts, which wasn't a long drive. When I got there, my daughter, who was 10 at the time, came running up to the car. She said, "Daddy, why are you so late?" But then she looked at me. By this time, all the sweat had come out of me. My shirt and pants were totally soaked from sweat.

My daughter went and got the adults, and they called the ambulance. I couldn't speak. The stroke had attacked my vocal system, and I had nothing to say. The ambulance took me to Prince George's Hospital, where doctors ran some tests. They said afterward that I had broken a blood vessel in my head, but they could administer some medication. I stayed there two or three days. Then I moved to the National Rehabilitation Hospital up on Michigan Avenue in Washington, DC.

Starting From Zero

I was in the rehab hospital for about two weeks. It was really tough. They got us up about 6:00 in the morning. We ate and then went to classes from about 8:00 a.m. to around lunchtime. Then we had classes from 1:30 p.m. to about 4:00 p.m. These classes would cover all kinds of therapy – speech therapy and things to help me with my stroke.

From 5:00 to 9:00 p.m. we had visiting hours. I was extremely tired after going through all the workouts. I'm a native Washingtonian, and when I'd finish my classes I'd find a roomful of people waiting for me. Within two weeks, 84 people came to visit me. By the time 9:00 came, I was totally exhausted.

On Sundays, you could go to church. I couldn't talk or anything, but I thought I could at least read my favorite scriptures. I looked at my Bible but I couldn't understand a word on the page. I couldn't read. I couldn't write. I couldn't talk. I couldn't walk. I was in a bad way. I couldn't communicate with anyone outside of myself. I could either laugh or cry. I decided to laugh about it.

ARRESTED: From Bad Habits to Breakthrough

Keeping the Faith

I finally got out of the rehab hospital and took therapy classes closer to my home in Mitchellville. I eventually mastered all the things they wanted me to master, but what helped my condition was that I had complete confidence in Someone higher than myself to take over my stroke and get me through it. I never lost faith. That's why I got better.

I watched a lot of people with strokes, and a lot of them didn't have anything to hold on to. They began to have problems with their strokes, new complications, and they died. I had to figure out what to do so I wouldn't have complications and die. I believe my faith, my belief in God, was a tremendous asset in kicking the stroke.

Recovery took a long time. I didn't start talking until about two months after the initial stroke. Because I'm a psychologist, I knew what to do when depression moved in on me. If I began to feel down, I would immediately shift my thinking to something more positive. I wouldn't let myself gather around negative thoughts.

You need patience to recover from a stroke. You can't rush through it. You can only do things when God says you're ready. You feel like you can make your leg move, but you can't. I didn't rush my recovery. I just waited until it was time to move a limb, and then I moved it.

Learning to Talk Again

Without my wife and my daughter, I wouldn't have recovered. They had to take over everything that I did before the stroke.

Tony Leaner

They were the two biggest helpers I had. I couldn't even tie my shoes. My daughter had to reach down and tie my shoes for me every morning. I definitely felt helpless – but I knew I would get out of that helpless mode as soon as I possibly could.

I also couldn't talk for two months – and nobody liked the fact that I couldn't talk better than my wife. I couldn't talk, so I couldn't say no. She had a good time with that.

The best thing my friends did for me was come around and talk. They talked all the time. I would listen to them talk and watch how they moved their lips, which helped my speech therapy. Talking was important, and I was a good listener. I relearned how to talk while they were sitting there talking about everything. I needed about two years to speak well enough for people to understand me. Within four years, I could speak comprehensively.

Thank goodness my reading comprehension came back to me about a year after the stroke. As I continued working with the therapists, the reading came back on its own.

A Halt on Stress

When I was in the rehab hospital, the doctor came and sat on my bed. He said, "Dr. McKenzie, you don't have any incidence of stroke in your family, so we don't know what caused your stroke. You're going to have to figure out what to eliminate from your life and what to keep."

So I got rid of all the stress in my life. I called a halt to everything and rebuilt my life so stress isn't a factor. Prior to my stroke, everything stressed me out: the job, karate lessons, the classes I taught – a lot of things. I think the stress was a bit too much, and I had to account for that.

Today my schedule is pretty good. I retired from my old job as a school psychologist in Montgomery County schools in 2004. I tried to go back to my old job shortly after the stroke but I just wasn't ready. I couldn't perform the way I had before. I wandered around for about a year, then I got a job as a full-time psychology professor at Prince George's Community College.

I still do karate. I still swim. The only thing I stopped doing was playing tennis at a very high level. I don't play tennis anymore.

Within about six years of the stroke, I think I was back to normal. Today I'd say I'm 90 percent recovered. People meeting me for the first time probably wouldn't know I had a stroke unless I told them.

Lessons Learned

A stroke is a silent killer; I didn't have any warning signs. I always tell guys to go to the doctor as often as they need to go. Men should have those regular tests for blood pressure and things like that. I didn't have issues with going to the doctor prior to my health crisis, but with a stroke, you have no symptoms. So now I don't hesitate to go in for regular check-ups.

My friends followed my example and went to their doctors. They felt I was a good role model, and I've led them down the right path. They'll listen when I say, "Hey, you better go get that checked. Don't sit around and wait."

For me and my family, this experience has made us stronger believers. Not that our faith was lacking before, but we've grown immensely stronger because I had nothing until I starting rebuilding. I think about the stroke every year on my wife's birthday but I try not to dwell on those memories too long. Instead, I try to move forward.

ARRESTED: From Bad Habits to Breakthrough

Larry Bussell Interview

I was cutting the grass one day in 1996 when I felt chest pains. I didn't call the ambulance. I drove myself to the emergency room, and the medical staff ended up keeping me there. About two days later I had an angioplasty procedure to widen two clogged arteries. The surgeon also put in stents to help the arteries remain open.

After that procedure, the doctor laid out a treatment plan for me. I exercised and ate right, but as the years progressed I went back to my old habits. I thought I could just do more exercise rather than maintain the changes in my diet. My case was typical of most men in that we think we know more than the doctor.

Cookie Monster

My biggest problem was eating the wrong foods. I loved cookies. Cookies have a high fat content, so fat plus high blood pressure – I always had high blood pressure – those two things kept me at risk for coronary heart disease. Sometimes I'd hide the cookies from my wife. Or she would go look for a couple cookies for herself and they would be gone because I'd eaten them all.

So I essentially ignored the doctor's advice. I had checkups regularly, and the doctor would say, "Your blood pressure is high. You need to work on that." I'd just do more exercise. Rather than concentrate on my high blood pressure, I would focus more on exercise. I didn't take time to learn what high cholesterol really meant. I didn't take the time to look up what high blood pressure really meant.

I thought that if I exercised more, I would put pressure on my heart to function properly. The activity would rinse all of the cholesterol out of my bloodstream. That was my uneducated reasoning behind not really following the doctor's orders.

Repeat Offender

Seven years later my problem reoccurred because I didn't manage my risk factors. But this time my health crisis was more intense. In the middle of the night, I woke up with severe chest pains. The pains were so strong, I didn't want to move. I struggled to breathe. This time I called the ambulance, but because it was the Fourth of July weekend, it took the emergency medical technicians a long time to respond. I sat on the couch and held my chest. Then I took a bag and tried to breathe in it, trying to do my own resuscitation.

I went to emergency care in Ft. Washington, and then the emergency technicians took me to Walter Reed General Hospital in Washington, DC. I thought the doctor could do another angioplasty and put in another stent, but I had too much blockage. Instead, the surgeon had to do a bypass. But this time, I had three clogged arteries instead of two.

Lord, Why Me?

I felt helpless during my second recovery. I couldn't do what I wanted to do. I had been really active. I loved to walk and play sports, but after the heart surgery, my doctors told me to be cautious, so I didn't do anything. I had to rely on my neighbors to cut my grass. I even felt downhearted on my way home from the hospital. We had a two-door sedan, and I couldn't ride in the front seat, so I had to maneuver my way into the back, which is difficult after having your sternum cut open. Then I literally had to crawl out of the back seat of the car. That was a little bit depressing.

I kept feeling like, "Lord, why me, why me, why me?" And that's when I started to feel the depression come on. I happened to have a youth gospel group CD that we purchased from a local store. I played the CD, which had a hip-hop gospel sound, and the music just kind of ignited the spirit in me. I felt a surge of power. I felt like the spirit came over me to let me know I was going to be all right.

After I stopped focusing on the pity party, I really started to concentrate on my rehab. I got on the treadmill a few days after I got home from the hospital and started my recovery process. I didn't need a lot of attention from others because my recovery was smooth. I didn't have any problems at all.

My wife was with me during the exit interview with the doctor as he went over my nutritional needs. So when she shopped for me after my surgery, she bought the things I needed to have and didn't buy the things that were bad for me, like the cookies. I didn't want to let the cookies go, but I did.

Tony Leaner

Warning Signs

I tell men to take heed to the warnings. We get warnings on food packages. We hear about staying away from fried foods, but we think, no, it couldn't happen to me because I'm not a couch potato. We come up with all these reasons why those warnings don't apply to us.

So I advise men to pay attention. Take advantage of all the health screenings and health fairs, and just get a check up to see where you are.

I also modified my diet. Whenever I have fried foods now, it's fried in olive oil. I don't use any of the high-fat oils when I have fried foods. I don't eat as much meat as I used to. I used to love pork ribs and stuff like that. Rarely do I have pork now. When I do eat meat, I usually have either fish or chicken, and it's the chicken without the skin.

I've continued exercising. I recently got into cycling, and I'll go out three or four times a week. Each time I go, I ride anywhere from 16 to 24 miles. So that has been really helpful in keeping my blood pressure and cholesterol numbers down. They're well within the normal range because of my exercise and diet.

A Healthy Partnership

My wife used to go riding with me until she hurt her knee recently and had knee surgery. She hasn't been as active since her surgery. But whenever we adjust our diet, we do it together because the changes benefit both of us. For two or three months, for example, we'll eat a lot of vegetables, green vegetables, and cut out sugars, pastries and bread. We'll do that until we get our weight down, and then we will gradually add some things back in. I rarely eat pastries and cookies now. I try to avoid them as much as possible.

ARRESTED: From Bad Habits to Breakthrough

Van Whitfield Interview

I had just returned from a trip to Alaska in 2011. I coach high school basketball, and I own and operate a school. We had just come back from this great trip. As soon as we got back – and this kind of speaks to what my schedule was like before all of this happened – we came back on Sunday, and on Monday we got on a bus to go play a tournament in North Carolina.

We then played in West Virginia, Pennsylvania and New Jersey – all inside of a week. I got up that Monday and went to the school, but I had this cough I couldn't shake. I already had a condition called sarcoidosis, which can cause inflammation in the lungs, liver, skin or other tissues. However, it was in remission.

I went to urgent care for the cough, and everything still seemed to be calm. But the doctor wanted to Medevac me to the hospital because it looked like I was having a massive heart attack. My wife remembers that I was coughing up blood. Even the medical staff hadn't seen anything like this.

I was airlifted to the hospital, but turns out I didn't have a heart attack. I had a blockage. It was definitely a heart condition, but not as severe. I left the hospital two days later in the midst of a bad snowstorm. I called my wife, who was stuck out at her sister's house. She asked why I was at home, and I said, "Well, I was tired of being there." I had asked my pastor to bring me home.

That night was the worst night of my life.

Tony Leaner

Swine Flu

That night, all I could do was crawl back and forth to the bathroom. I couldn't even get in the bed. I was emaciated and dehydrated. I didn't know what was wrong.

When day broke, I called my wife to tell her to come home. She got home just after the ambulance arrived. I crawled downstairs so the emergency medical technicians wouldn't break down the door. There was too much snow for them to even get in the driveway, so they propped me up and walked me to the ambulance. That was the last thing I remember.

They took me to the hospital. The doctors told my wife they would put me in a coma because I wouldn't make it through the night. At least the family would be able to see me because I'd still be alive technically.

By the time more of my family arrived, my situation had grown worse, so they moved me from Prince George's Hospital Center to the University of Maryland up in Baltimore. That's where they found out what was wrong: I had swine flu.

At Death's Door

By that time I had contracted pneumonia. My lung had collapsed. I had respiratory distress syndrome and congestive heart failure. I had maybe seven different things that could independently kill a person. During the course of my illness, I flatlined three times. I was on life support.

I stayed in that coma for an entire month. When they

would bring me out, I wouldn't know what was going on. I thought I had just arrived at the hospital and was on my way out. No one could visit but family and clergy.

When I came out of the first coma, I didn't know anything. The hospital staff asked questions to assess my mental state. They would ask, "Do you know who you are?" I'd say, "No, ma'am." They would ask, "Do you know what month it is?" I would say, "Tuesday."

At that point, they put me in another coma and placed me on dialysis for 24 hours a day for about three weeks. I had complete kidney as well as liver failure. Every organ just shut down.

Five other people were in intensive care with me who had swine flu. All five of those people died.

A Marathon in One Step

I was in intensive care for four months. The bill for February alone was like $300,000. I was 51, and I'd never had insurance most of my adult life. My wife, however, had insisted that I get insurance when we got married in November 2010. The insurance took effect January 1, 2011. I got sick January 26.

I left the hospital and went to a nursing home. The staff set up an aggressive therapy for me, but they told me I'd never walk again. I would be on oxygen the rest of my life and might never eat again. I'd lost 80 pounds by that point and my muscles had atrophied.

I stayed in the nursing home four months. I was the youngest person there. Seeing 90-year-old people do things that I couldn't do wore me down mentally. I couldn't do anything but go to therapy and lie in the bed.

When I left there, we had to move into a one-bedroom apartment in Alexandria because my beautiful 6,000-square foot home in Lake Arbor had too many steps. I was on oxygen in a wheelchair. I had gone from being an active person who had been to Alaska, West Virginia and Philadelphia within a two-week period to a person who couldn't get out of bed to go to the bathroom.

My physical therapist wanted me to accept that my old life was gone. But when the therapist would leave, I would get up and try to walk. I would fall, but I kept saying, "I have to walk." Eventually I took a step. My heart only operated at like 10 percent; in fact, I thought I'd have to get a heart transplant. So taking a step was like running a marathon. Recovering from that one step took forever. But six weeks later, I could walk.

One day my oxygen mask fell off while I was asleep. When you're on oxygen, you think you can't live without it. But when I realized my mask was off, I didn't panic like I usually did. I just stopped using it.

I Saw My Casket

Today I'm off oxygen. I walk and exercise every day. I'm probably 95 percent to 97 percent recovered. I still have pain in my legs and feet, and I'm recovering from an episode of gout. But I'm happy to be alive.

When I flatlined and died back in the hospital, I knew I had died. All those things people say about near-death experiences – the white light – I remember that. I saw my casket. I saw my headstone. That changes you. People can't intimidate me. I've seen what death looks like, and nothing is scarier than that.

I tell men to get checkups, take care of their health and pray like crazy. The main thing is just to give your life over. We feel like it's a weakness to surrender our lives to anything, to allow ourselves to be powerless. Actually, you get strength when you understand that there's a much bigger force that's going to take care of everything. Even if you don't make it, He'll take care of those left behind. If God can reach back and save me, you need to appreciate Him for the simple things. If He did it for me, He can do it for you.

This is All God

I go back to the hospital frequently to thank the staff members and bring them gifts. The hospital personnel can't believe I survived. They don't even recognize me. They say, "Well, if you lie down and put a bunch of tape over your face and a tube in your throat, we'll know it's you."

I've had doctors in tears because they say, "There's no way you can be alive." I was in the room that no one ever comes out of alive. They keep that room dark. Every other room is brightly lit, but that room – it's a corner room – is dark, even when I go up to visit the hospital staff today. They assumed when I left that unit that I had died or I was going someplace else, like hospice, to die.

My primary care physician said, "Never let any doctor take credit for this. This is all God." My heart, for example, shouldn't have recovered. When I was at 10 percent functionality, the best improvement I could hope for is 20 percent. That alone would have been a miracle. My heart is back to about 60 percent.

When I went to see my cardiologist recently, he had an intern with him. He told the intern, "This patient right here is why you get involved in medicine – because you want to see a miracle." He told me, "We did the best we could do medically, but if anyone ever doubts there is a God, this is proof. There is nothing we can point to that says this is why this man survived and appears to have a normal life."

In Closing

Somebody reading this book felt a pain recently –- maybe even today. And you discounted it by saying, "Oh, it's just heartburn," or "Oh, it's just acid reflux."

I urge you to get checked out by a doctor. In my case, a major, life-threatening event had to occur to get me on the path of taking responsibility for my health. That doesn't have to be your story. As I heard someone say: We have to own our own health. If we don't care enough about ourselves, then who should or who can?

Many of us have a foolish, careless attitude about our health until we get ARRESTED. An unexpected illness locks us in handcuffs and tries us in the court of health. We have no defense. Our own poor choices cause us pain, cost us time and money, and force us to depend on others for the most basic needs. Some men lose their lives, leaving behind grieving families and unfinished goals and dreams.

I pray that something presented in this book prompts you to be more proactive and responsible. I'm not saying I got it all figured out. This health thing is a daily challenge. And to complicate things even more, if we just keep living, time or age could eventually cause us to experience health problems. There are no guarantees.

Even so, we're likely to enjoy better quality of life into old age if we follow some simple common-sense approaches. Get a physical. Drink more water. Walk for 30 minutes three days a week. Follow the doctor's advice regarding your medications or chronic conditions. Eat more fruits and veggies. Quit smoking. Prevention is the key.

In the end, it's all up to you. So are you in? Is it time to make a change? Or does an emergency room doctor have to deliver some bad news to get you to do the right thing? I think the answer to that question is NO!!

We're strong enough in our will and conviction to arrest our bad habits one by one, day by day, before our bad habits arrest us.

Put out an arrest warrant on those bad habits today so you or someone you love can escape death row and get a reduced sentence -- one that allows for a long, fruitful life!

RESOURCES

Tex was a good friend of mine who died about two years ago. For a long time Tex complained of not feeling well. It seemed that Tex didn't have much of an appetite. He also complained a lot about not being able to keep food down. These complaints went on for what seems like a year.

Finally a few of us insisted that he go to the hospital. When he did, he discovered that he had a rare form of cancer in his esophagus. He started getting some treatments; however, by this time the cancer had progressed to stage four, and Tex died a short time later. When I asked him why he waited so long to get himself checked out, he simply said that his procrastination all boiled down to the fact that he didn't have insurance.

So in memory of Tex, here are resources available to anyone regardless of whether you have insurance or not. If you're sick and without health care coverage, the law says that you can't be denied care. That's right: It's against the law for a public hospital facility to refuse to care for you or deny your admittance simply for the lack of health insurance coverage. So if you're not feeling well, go to the emergency room of any public hospital and get the care need.

Tony Leaner

The Affordable Care Act

In the summer of 2012, The Supreme Court passed its decision to uphold the Affordable Care Act. The "vast majority" of Americans will not be affected by the Court's ruling. If you have health insurance you're unaffected. If you can't afford insurance you're unaffected. It's only for those who can afford healthcare but choose not to have it; they will now have to pay a penalty.

Starting in 2014, most people will be required to have health insurance or pay a penalty if they don't. Coverage may include employer-provided insurance, coverage someone buys on their own, or Medicaid. Americans without health insurance will be required to get covered or pay a fine (1% of income in 2014 and increasing to 2.5% in 2016). Subsidies will be provided for those who can't afford it and businesses with over 50 employees will face fines if they don't offer coverage to their workers.

Once the Affordable Care Act is implemented, Americans can no longer be denied insurance because of preexisting conditions or have their insurance revoked or their premiums jump because they get sick. "This law will...end discrimination in the insurance market" through the individual mandate, which will bring everyone into the health insurance market.

Several groups are exempt from the requirement to obtain coverage or pay the penalty, including: people who would have to pay more than 8 percent of their income for health insurance, people with incomes below the threshold required for filing taxes (in 2009, $9,350 for a single person and $26,000 for a married couple with two children), those who qualify for religious exemptions, undocumented immigrants, people who are incarcerated, and members of Indian tribes.

IN THE MEANTIME... Be assured that emergency service will never be delayed or withheld on the basis of a patient's ability to pay. If you do not have health insurance, you should contact the hospital's financial counselor. The financial counselor will review payment and funding options that may be available to you. These could include applying for Medicaid, Family Care programs, bank financing, extended payment plans and charity care considerations.

Things You Should Know...

What are my options for job-based coverage?

If you don't have coverage, you may be eligible for health insurance coverage through work – your own job or that of your spouse or parent. If an employer offers coverage, you generally can't be turned away or charged a higher premium because of your health status or disability. This protection is called "nondiscrimination."

Employers may refuse or restrict coverage for other reasons (such as part-time employment), as long as these are unrelated to your health status and are applied consistently. For more information, contact the Employee Benefits

Security Administration, U.S. Department of Labor at 1-866-444-3272 or visit www.askebsa.dol.gov.

What are my options if I can't get coverage through work?

If you can't get insurance through your or your spouse's employer, you have a number of options:

Insurance Under a Parent's Policy: If you are under 26, you may be eligible for coverage under your parent's insurance policy.

Individual Insurance Policies: If you cannot get health insurance through work, you may be able to buy a health insurance policy for yourself or your family. Be aware that policies are often expensive, and that until 2014 you can be charged more, be rejected for coverage, or have your coverage restricted due to a health condition or other factors.

Pre-Existing Condition Insurance Plan: If you have a pre-existing health condition and have been uninsured for the past six months, you may qualify for the Pre-Existing Condition Insurance Plan (PCIP) created under the Affordable Care Act.

Medicaid: Each state operates a Medicaid program that provides health coverage for lower-income people, families and children, the elderly, and people with disabilities. The eligibility rules for Medicaid are different for each state, but most states offer coverage for adults with children at some income level.

Beginning in 2014, most adults under age 65 with individual incomes up to about $15,000 per year will qualify for Medicaid in every state.

Free or low-cost care: If you are unable to afford insurance coverage, there are health clinics in your community that provide free or reduced-cost services on a sliding scale, depending on your income.

Ask doctors to cut your bill: No one pays the sticker price for health care except, paradoxically, uninsured people who don't have the benefit of the big discounts that public and private insurers negotiate on behalf of their members. Many doctors will offer a similar discount to uninsured people paying bills, especially those paying at the time of treatment, but you have to ask.

Comparison shop for prescription drugs: You can easily end up paying more than you need to by, say, failing to compare prices at more than one pharmacy, or taking an expensive brand-name drug when a cheaper generic could work just as well.

Take advantage of health fairs: Many community groups periodically run health fairs that include free screenings for such conditions as hearing loss, high blood pressure, and high cholesterol. Some also offer free flu shots and vision screenings.

Look for disease-specific programs: There are dozens of them but you have to know where to look and, in many cases, follow some very specific rules. But to qualify in many states, your condition must have been diagnosed at one of the program's approved screening centers. If you received a diagnosis elsewhere, you're not eligible.

Apply for free or reduced-price hospital care: Many facilities have programs for people who are struggling financially. But it can be a challenge looking for charitable assistance and applying for it. The Affordable Care Act has several provisions designed to help uninsured or underinsured patients who can't afford hospital care. The law says that all nonprofit hospitals must develop a written policy on financial assistance, including information on who is eligible and how to apply, which they must make "widely available" to the public.

Start with the hospital billing office, social worker, or patient representative. I f you don't get satisfactory results the first time, keep trying. Hospital staff members might not know about the policy, even though they're supposed to.

Go to a community health center: There are more than 8,000 across the country. They provide basic outpatient care—including, in some cases, dental and mental-health services—and they charge according to a person's ability to pay.

What if I'm losing work-based coverage?
COBRA Coverage
If you're losing your work-based coverage because you're leaving your job, you may have the option of keeping the coverage through a program called COBRA.

COBRA is a federal law that may let you keep employee health insurance for a limited time after your employment ends or after you would otherwise lose coverage. This is called "continuation coverage."

Since your employer doesn't pay for COBRA coverage, you'll probably pay for the whole cost of the monthly premium.

Here's what you need to know about COBRA coverage:
In general, COBRA coverage requirements apply only to employers with 20 or more employees. (Many states have laws similar to COBRA that apply to employers with fewer than 20 employees. Contact your State Department of Insurance to see if "state continuation coverage" applies to you.)

If your family was covered under your employer coverage, they may also qualify for COBRA coverage.
In most situations, you should get a notice from your employer's benefits administrator or the health plan telling you that your coverage is ending and offering you the right to take COBRA coverage.

In most cases, you have 60 days after your last day of coverage to sign up for COBRA. COBRA coverage usually lasts for 18 months but could last up to 36 months.

Tony Leaner

For more information about COBRA coverage:

Call your employer's benefits administrator for questions about your specific COBRA coverage options.

If your health plan coverage was from a private employer (not a government employer), you can visit the Department of Labor's Web site, or call 1-866-444-3272.

If your health plan coverage was from a state or local government employer, you can call 1-877-267-2323, extension 61565.

If your coverage was through employment with the federal government, you can visit the Office of Personnel Management's Web site at www.opm.gov.

"Conversion" Coverage and HIPAA-Eligible Coverage
When you're leaving job-based coverage, you might be able to convert your job-based health insurance plan to an individual policy. This is called "conversion" coverage, and isn't the same as "continuation coverage" (COBRA), in which you keep your job-based coverage. If you have a choice, you should consider your options carefully. You might also have special rights to buy individual coverage as a "HIPAA eligible individual."

Contact your State Department of Insurance to see if these coverage options are available to you.

Cancer

What can you do if you suspect you may have cancer, but don't have health insurance?

If your cancer is slow-growing and non-emergent in nature, you could sign up for health insurance (or get a job with health insurance benefits) and wait until after the pre-existing condition exclusion period to have it discovered by your doctor. So long as you don't know you have cancer and you have not sought medical attention to diagnose or treat the cancer, it might not be considered a pre-existing condition.

Some health insurance plans will require a physical or blood test before issuing a policy. (This is more common with life insurance than health insurance policies.) Such examinations, however, might not detect the cancer if it is not palpable. This approach, however, is risky for two reasons. First, delaying treatment could have serious consequences for your health. Second, failing to disclose your condition could involve fraud.

An alternative is to seek immediate treatment and talk to a social worker at the hospital about ways to pay for the treatment. The hospital's billing department may be able to set up a payment plan, or discount the bills to the "usual and customary" charges paid by insurance companies. The hospital may have a community care program that helps needy patients with their bills. If you're indigent, you might qualify for Medicaid. Pharmaceutical companies have established compassionate drug programs such as NeedyMeds and Partnership for Prescription Assistance (1-888-4PPA-NOW).

State Sponsored Programs for Maryland
These programs provide assistance for those who want to get their medications through patient assistance programs. All are free or charge a small amount. Most help people in limited geographic areas.

Kidney Disease Program of Maryland
- Medical assistance for those with End Stage Renal Disease.

MADAP-Plus
- Health Insurance Payment Assistance; helps people with HIV/AIDS pay health insurance premiums, deductibles, etc.

Maryland AIDS Drug Assistance Program (MADAP) (a/k/a ADAP)
- AIDS drug assistance program

Maryland Health Coverage Tax Credit
- Bridge Program; pays 72.5% of health insurance premiums while you wait for Federal HCTC approval

Maryland Health Insurance Plan (MHIP)/ Pre-Existing Condition Insurance Plan
- Health insurance program for those unable to obtain

insurance from other sources

Maryland Medical Assistance (Maryland Medicaid)
- Comprehensive health care for the needy.

Partners for Health Improvement Program (Partners.H.I.P.)
- Full health care coverage at a discounted cost

Primary Adult Care Program (PAC)
- Health services for low-income individuals age 19 and over

Public Health Dentistry
- Dental services with fees based on income

Respite Care Services - Maryland DDA
- Financial assistance for respite care

Senior Health Insurance Assistance Program (SHIP)
- Your local help with Medicare

Senior Prescription Drug Assistance Program (SPDAP)
- Financial assistance to residents enrolled in an approved Medicare prescription drug plan.

Sexually Transmitted Disease Prevention Program Caroline St.
- Free test for HIV or other sexually transmitted infections.

Tony Leaner

Sexually Transmitted Disease Prevention Program
North Ave.
- Free test for HIV or other sexually transmitted infections

ONLINE RESOURCES

http://www.healthcare.gov
Learn about the benefits of the health care law where you live.

http://finder.healthcare.gov/
- To look for a private insurance plan
- To learn whether there are additional insurance plans for residents with pre-existing health conditions in your state
- To learn more about your state Medicaid program and other options available to you
- To learn more about coverage for children and other options available to you

http://www.healthcare.gov/using-insurance/low-cost-care/medicaid/index.html
- Medicaid provides coverage for people with lower incomes, older people, people with disabilities, and some families and children.

http://www.needymeds.com
- NeedyMeds is a 501(c)(3) non-profit information resource devoted to helping people in need find assistance programs to help them afford their medications and costs related to health care.

http://www.pparx.org
- The Partnership for Prescription Assistance helps qualifying patients without prescription drug coverage

to get the medicines they need through the program that is right for them. Many will get their medications free or nearly free. They will help you find the program that's right for you, free of charge.

http://www.healthcare.gov/law/features/choices/pre-existing-condition-insurance-plan/index.html
- To learn more about the Pre-Existing Condition Insurance Plan.

http://cobrahealthinsurance.com/Health_Insurance_Unisurable_State_risk_pools.html
- If you find that you're uninsurable due to pre-existing conditions, try contacting one of the Health Insurance Risk Pools in certain states.

http://cobrahealthinsurance.com/Resource/Maryland_Cobra_Health_Insurance.html
- The ultimate resource for COBRA insurance information and options in Maryland.

http://findahealthcenter.hrsa.gov/Search_HCC.aspx
- Federally funded health centers care for you, even if you have no health insurance. You pay what you can afford, based on your income.

http://www.dol.gov/ebsa/publications/yhphipaa.html
- Your rights and protections under health insurance through your job.

http://www.healthcare.gov/law/features/choices/young-adult-coverage/index.html
- Under the Affordable Care Act, if your plan covers children, you can now add or keep your children on your health insurance policy until they turn 26 years old.

http://www.naic.org/ (Then click on the header "States and Jurisdiction Map")
- To see if continuation coverage options (such as "Conversion" and HIPAA Coverage) are available to you.